THE WATCHERS ON THE WALL COLLECTION

Heavenly FATHER

Book of Scripture Prayers
for Everyday Life

Glenn Bongard

© 2021 by Glenn Bongard

All rights reserved. No part of this book may be reproduced or transmitted in any form or by any means, electronic or mechanical, including photography and recording, or by any information storage or retrieval system, except as may be expressly permitted in writing by the publisher. The only exception is brief quotations in printed reviews.

Scripture quotations marked (NLT) are taken from the Holy Bible, New Living Translation, copyright ©1996, 2004, 2015 by Tyndale House Foundation. Used by permission of Tyndale House Publishers, Carol Stream, Illinois 60188. All rights reserved.

Scripture quotations marked (TLB) are taken from The Living Bible copyright © 1971. Used by permission of Tyndale House Publishers, Carol Stream, Illinois 60188. All rights reserved.

Scripture quotations marked (The Message) are taken from THE MESSAGE, copyright © 1993, 2002, 2018 by Eugene H. Peterson. Used by permission of NavPress, represented by Tyndale House Publishers. All rights reserved.

Scripture quotations marked (MEV) taken from the Modern English Version. Copyright © 2014 by Military Bible Association. Used by permission. All rights reserved.

Scripture quotations marked (NKJV) taken from the New King James Version®. Copyright © 1982 by Thomas Nelson. Used by permission. All rights reserved.

THE HOLY BIBLE, NEW INTERNATIONAL VERSION®, NIV® Copyright © 1973, 1978, 1984, 2011 by Biblica, Inc.™ Used by permission. All rights reserved worldwide.

Cover Photography by Glenn Bongard

The photograph was taken at Cliff Mine Road, North of Calumet, Michigan

ISBN 9798730368330 *(paperback)*

Published by Purposed Publishing

www.purposedpublishing.com

Introduction

In 2012, my pastor preached a sermon about turning your misery into your ministry. This jolted me and caused me to reevaluate how my life was going at the time. I was struggling spiritually because I was fighting anger, for changes on my job that led to an hour increase in my commute. I was still teaching but I wanted to move up to being a principal and I had lost my coaching job. Life was not going as I had planned.

I accepted my pastor's challenge. I emailed him and asked for the names of all the married couples in our church so I could start to pray over them as well as the church's leadership team and their children. He sent me fifty couples to start praying over. As I began interceding for those on my list each day, God started to change my heart and my view on prayer. I started researching every book I could get my hands on about prayer.

April 18, 2017, I started, at the request of a pastor's wife, to lead five friends in praying Scripture over their families.

Heavenly Father

We prayed together faithfully for almost a year until the Holy Spirit told me to stop. Then in 2018, I started an email ministry of praying over two pastors with a group of about thirty people which grew over time. Monday through Friday, I would send out two email prayers, using Scripture, praying over these pastors. During that time I started to see God move in ways I never expected. I also started to put together Scripture prayers for different areas of life.

In 2019, my email list of thirty people grew to over 150 as I was invited by my denomination to pray for the pastors in my local conference. People joined with me to pray for pastors, church requests, and personal petitions that were sent to me.

Over these years, I compiled many scriptural prayers for different areas of life. These faithful prayers over the years laid the foundation for the book you're holding in your hands.

Then on March 25, 2020, at 6 o'clock at night, I went to my study and found my youngest son had died from a gunshot wound to the head. I still don't know if it was an accident or suicide, but I do know I had lost my miracle son who had just turned twenty-one, eight days earlier. I had no choice but to stop sending out prayers. I needed to take the time to find God and myself. I had to wrestle with my faith and process my grief with God. In the midst of that pain, God met me there.In December of 2020, the Holy Spirit told me to start writing a Scripture prayer from each book of the Bible. I was obedient and, eighteen days later, I was finished! Through this gradual healing process, I have started emailing prayers again. I even organized all my scripture prayers into packets and sent them out to see if anyone would publish them. God inspired me to send my three copies to Jacquetta Dantzler and she has worked tirelessly to put these into book form.

I pray that these Scripture prayers will assist you in learning to pray deeper and ignite a passion within you for God and His Word.

Table of Contents

1. Following Jesus 1
2. Using the Lord's Prayer as a Guide 4
3. Learning to Forgive 7
4. Growing in Faith 10
5. Wearing the Armor of God 13
6. Mind and Spirit 17
7. Hurting and Broken 21
8. God's Protection 26
9. Adult Children 28
10. Family Discipleship 30
11. Walking in Love 32
12. Living a Holy Life 35
13. Troubles and Suffering 39
14. Standing on God's Word 42
15. The Body of Christ 44
16. The Church 47
17. School Districts 49

18 Pursuing Wisdom	52
19 Joy in the Face of Trials	55
20 Obedience to God	59
21 Producing Good Fruit	61
22 An Athlete's Prayer	67
23 Exercising your Body	69
24 Handling Money	71
25 Physical and Mental Health	73
26 Leading People	75
Scriptures from Footnotes	78

1
Following Jesus

Heavenly Father, thank You for creating me and desiring a relationship with me.

Holy Spirit, let the words I use, the thoughts I ponder, the dreams I dream and the desires I focus on, be aligned with Your plans for me and the desires You seek to instill in me.[1]

Help me to seek daily Your wisdom, listen for Your voice of guidance, and discern Your perfect will.[2]

Holy Spirit, help me to realize You walk with me, protect me, and comfort me. You help me to see life for what it truly is. Open my eyes to Your wisdom and guidance found in the testimonies You put in the Bible. Give me a desire to learn from the lessons You taught, the principles You gave, and the

---

1 Psalm 19:14
2 Proverbs 2:1-6; Romans 12:2

Heavenly Father

expectations the New Testament writers penned. Help me to correctly divide the Word so I can gain wisdom, purpose, and focus.

Lord, lead me to live a life that is full of doing Your will and responding to You.[3]

Teach me to serve others so they can see You in me. Remind me to daily seek my very sustenance from what You provide. Show me who You are and who I am in You.[4]

Lead me as I attempt to walk with determination, confidence, and joy on the path You have placed me on.[5]

Allow me to help others find their way to this path so they can begin their journey towards Your Kingdom. Help me to stand before others and be so reflective of who You are, that they see You and not me. Let me rejoice with those who rejoice, weep with those who weep[6], and be compassionate to all for Your glory.

Create within me the ability to breathe in life from Your Word, Spirit, and wisdom and to breathe out Your love,

---

3   James 1:22
4   Hebrews 11:6
5   Proverbs 3:5-6
6   Romans 12:15

grace, and mercy to others. Help me to be bold in my faith in who You are and what You are molding me into being.

Thank You for giving Your all to create, save, and offer a relationship to me. Now help me to give my all to You so I can become what You created me to be and to be completely fulfilled in my life here on earth. Teach me to be grateful for Your instruction, discipline, and guidance, during hard times, as well as the good times.

In Jesus' name, Amen.

2
Using the Lord's Prayer as a Guide

Our Father in Heaven, hallowed be Your name, Your Kingdom come, Your will be done on earth as it is in Heaven. Give us today our daily bread. Forgive us our debts, as we also have forgiven our debtors. And lead us not into temptation, but deliver us from the evil one.[7]

Lord, help me to love You with all my heart and with all my soul and with all my mind and with all my strength.[8] I glorify You because you are able to keep me from falling away and You graciously bring me into Your glorious presence. All glory, majesty, power, and authority belong to You, my Savior, Jesus Christ.[9] O Lord, You are my God; I will exalt You

---

7   Matthew 6:9-13
8   Jude 24-25 (NLT)
9   Isaiah 25:1

and praise Your name, for in perfect faithfulness you have done marvelous things, things planned long ago.

Your Kingdom come, Your Will be done on earth as it is in Heaven.[10] Because of Your goodness God, I offer my body as a living sacrifice. As I worship You, I ask that You would transform me by renewing my mind. Reveal to me Your Will— Your good, pleasing, and perfect Will[11], that I might preach Your good news with my actions, as well as my words. Lord, You said that signs would accompany those who believed, so I pray that You would empower me to do the miraculous.[12]

Give us today our daily bread.[13] Lord, thank You that You are my provider and that I have no need to fear about the future. You clothe the flowers of the field and You give food to the birds, yet You care for me even more than they, so I will choose to look to You to satisfy me. I trust You with my cares for today and my worries about tomorrow and choose to seek Your Kingdom and Your righteousness first and foremost.[14] I choose to rejoice in You, Lord because You are near. I lay my anxieties before You and ask that You would grant me Your peace that surpasses all understanding.Forgive us

---

10   Romans 12:1-2
11   Mark 16:15-18
12   Mark 16:20
13   Luke 12:22-31
14   Philippians 4:4-7

our debts, as we also have forgiven our debtors.[15] Jesus, thank You, that You have forgiven me. Holy Spirit, empower me to forgive those who have sinned against me, that I might reflect You to the world around me.

And lead us not into temptation, but deliver us from the evil one.[16] Lord, thank You for the justification You provided through Christ's sacrifice. I rejoice in the hope, grace, and peace You have graciously lavished upon me. Even in the midst of trials and tribulations, keep my focus on You and You alone. Lord, direct my heart into the depths of Your love for me.[17]

In Jesus' name, Amen.

---

15 John 20:21-23
16 Romans 5:1-5
17 2 Thessalonians 3:5

3

Learning to Forgive

Heavenly Father, I praise You for the life of Christ, as recorded in Scripture, that teaches me how to live in the salvation He granted through His obedience. I know I must forgive others in order to be forgiven as Jesus spoke of when He said, "And when you stand praying, forgive if you have anything against anyone, so that your Father who is in heaven may also forgive you of your sins. But if you do not forgive, neither will your Father who is in heaven forgive your sins."[18]

Paul teaches that I should forgive "lest Satan should take advantage of us. For we are not ignorant of his devices."[19]

Lord, help me to be a good steward of the grace You have freely offered to me. Fill me to overflowing with Your love,

---

18   Mark 11:25
19   2 Corinthians 2:11

because Your love covers a multitude of sins. Help me use my gifts to serve others so that You may be glorified in me.[20]

Help me to learn to forgive, love, and live as peaceably as I can with all people. Empower me to stand firm in my belief and faith of Christ's forgiveness and salvation so that I can be an example to unbelievers.

Holy Spirit, help me stay out of the judging business and keep me focused on living a holy and loving life. Teach me to search my heart daily and harbor no unforgiveness. Give me wisdom in who I associate with and give me a desire to forgive.

Keep me from fear, hatred, and bitterness in the midst of trials and tribulations in this broken world. Remind me constantly of Your grace and protect me from the weapons of Satan that would try to pull me away from You.

Help me continually work out my salvation with fear and trembling, knowing that it is You who are working in me. May Your will be done in my life and may my actions bring You pleasure.[21]

---

20   1 Peter 4:7-11
21   Philippians 2:12-13

Lord, direct my heart into deeper levels of Your love and the patience of Christ as I am obedient to forgive others as You have forgiven me.[22]

In Jesus' name, Amen.

---

22   2 Thessalonians 3:5

# 4

Growing in Faith

Oh Lord, You are my strength, my rock, my fortress, and my deliverer; I take refuge in You and You are my shield, my salvation, and my stronghold.[23]

Jesus, You taught that if anyone says to this mountain, "Go, throw yourself into the sea" and does not doubt in his heart but believes that what he says will happen, it will be done for him.[24] Help me to believe with this kind of faith so I can move mountains in my life that are in the way.

Lord, I know that it's impossible to please You without faith. I believe that You are God and that You reward those who diligently seek You.[25] Help me to seek You with faith greater than a mustard seed so that I can please You!

---

23 Psalm 18:1-2
24 Mark 11:23
25 Hebrews 11:6

Matthew 21:22 records that whatever we ask you in prayer, believing, we will receive.[26] Knowing this, I ask that You continue to reveal who You are. Empower me to seek Your will, Your heart, and Your righteousness above all else.

Jesus, you promised in Mark 16:17-18 that, "these signs will accompany those who believe: In my name, they will drive out demons; they will speak in new tongues; they will pick up snakes with their hands; and when they drink deadly poison, it will not hurt them at all; they will place their hands on sick people, and they will get well."[27] Lord, help me to find this kind of faith so people can be saved. Help me to pray with a faith that can drive Satan and his demons away. Give me the faith to lay hands on people so You can heal them and be glorified.

Fill me with faith like Shadrach, Meshach, and Abednego had in Daniel 3. Holy Spirit, I believe that you are able to do anything, but even when you don't move as I expect, I will continue to trust you. I place my faith in you, regardless of outcome or circumstances. Give me unwavering confidence in you, as David did when he wrote, Psalms 116:2, "Because He turned His ear to me I will call on Him as long as I live."[28]

---

26 Matthew 21:22
27 Mark 16:17-18
28 Psalm 116:2

I thank you that, "The eyes of the Lord are on the righteous and His ears are attentive to their prayers."[29] Lord, remind me that I am righteous in Christ, so I can have confidence that You hear me. Help me bear Your fruit of love, joy, peace, patience, kindness, goodness, faithfulness, gentleness, and self-control.[30] And help me live by Your Spirit and keep in step with Your Spirit.[31] Lord, help me to seek and cherish wisdom so that I can understand and discern Your Will in my life. Increase my faith and teach me Your voice that I may always be listening and ready to respond when You speak.

In Jesus' name, Amen.

---

29 1 Peter 3:12
30 Galatians 5:22-23
31 Galatians 5:25

5
Wearing the Armor of God

I will exalt you, my God and King; I will praise Your name forever and ever. Every day I will praise You and extol Your name forever and ever. Great is the Lord and most worthy of praise; Your greatness no one can fathom. One generation will commend Your works to another; they will tell of Your mighty acts. They will speak of the glorious splendor of Your majesty, and I will meditate on Your wonderful works.[32]

Holy Spirit I ask that You put a hedge of protection around my family as You did for Job[33]. Increase my faith and teach me Your voice that I may always be listening and ready to respond when You speak. Help me to glean wisdom from Your Word and apply it to my life so I can navigate the path You have chosen for me. Holy Spirit, help me to be strong

---

32 Psalm 145:1-5
33 Job 1:10

Heavenly Father

in the Lord and in His mighty power. Help me to put on the full armor of God today so that I can stand against the devil's schemes. Remind me that my struggle is not against flesh and blood, but against the rulers, authorities, powers of this dark world, and the spiritual forces of evil in the heavenly realms.

Prepare me to stand my ground when evil comes. Let me stand firm with the belt of truth buckled around my waist. The belt of truth is my foundation, it holds the tools of wisdom, knowledge, and discernment close to my side to help me make wise decisions.

Let me put on the breastplate of righteousness so that my heart and lungs are protected. This way I will treasure Your wisdom, Your word, and Your principles. I choose to breathe in Your Word and meditate on it so it circulates through my spirit, enabling me to exhale exhortation of wisdom, gentleness, compassion, truth, grace, and mercy onto the world around me.

Keep my feet always fitted with the readiness that comes from the gospel of peace. So I can always be ready to give an account of the hope that lies within me and assist the least of these.

Help me to take up and hold onto my shield of faith. Let it defend me from the lies of Satan and this world. Help me to use it to defend my trust in You and to let it be the barrier between me and hopelessness, depression, and sin.

Let me take up my helmet of salvation so all will know whose side I have chosen to be on. Also let it protect my thought life, my goals, my meditations, and my understanding of Your word and principles.

Finally, let me use the sword of the Spirit so that I pray on all occasions with all kinds of prayers and requests. Help me to be alert and always praying for the saints. Help me to wield the faith of a mustard seed to move mountains and giants out of the way. Holy Spirit, I choose to listen to Your promptings, that I might show myself approved in rightly dividing Your Word.

Lord, thank You that I can live by faith. Though I am in the world, I am not of the world, so I don't need to use the world's tools to fight the good fight. Thank You for providing the weapons to engage in spiritual warfare—teach me how to use them well.

Thank You that I don't need to be afraid because You have given me the spirit of power, love, and a sound mind. If any thoughts in my mind are not of You, I ask that you make me aware of them so that I can tear down any thought and bring it into the obedience of Christ. Lord, thank You for Your Word, continue to correct, instruct, and equip me with it.

Heavenly Father

Continue to correct and instruct me as I grow in my relationship with You. Thank You for adopting me as an heir, remind me of this truth as I help build Your Kingdom here on Earth. Remind me that You fight my battles and that my hope rests in You. Finally, let the words of my mouth and the meditation of my heart be acceptable in Your sight, O Lord, my strength and my redeemer.[34]

In Jesus' precious name, Amen.

---

34 Ephesians 6:10-20, 2 Corinthians 5:7, 2 Corinthians 10:3-5, 2 Timothy 1:7, 2 Timothy 3:16-17, and Psalm 19:14

6
Mind and Spirit

"Sing joyfully to the Lord, you righteous;
    it is fitting for the upright to praise him.
Praise the Lord with the harp;
    make music to him on the ten-stringed lyre.
Sing to him a new song;
    play skillfully, and shout for joy.
For the word of the Lord is right and true;
    he is faithful in all he does.
The Lord loves righteousness and justice;
    the earth is full of his unfailing love."[35]

Holy Spirit, put a hedge of protection around my family to keep us safe from harm and evil. Thank You, Lord, for not condemning me for my sins. I'm grateful that You

---

35   Psalm 33:1-5

Heavenly Father

have offered me a way of escape by Christ paying the price on the cross for my sins.[36]

Today, I offer my body as a living sacrifice, holy and pleasing to You, as a spiritual act of worship. Help me not to conform to the pattern of this world, but be transformed by renewing my mind as I continually meditate on Your Word, so I can test and approve what Your will is Your good, pleasing and perfect will.[37]

Help my love to be sincere, and may I hate what is evil but cling to what is good. Help me devote my life to brotherly love, attempting to honor others above myself. Fill me with zeal and spiritual fervor as I serve You, O Lord. Allow me to learn to be joyful in hope, patient in affliction, faithful in prayer, and overflowing with hospitality. Help me to bless those who persecute me, and not curse. Fill me with compassion and empathy so I can rejoice with those who rejoice and mourn with those who mourn. I long to live a life of harmony with others. Keep me from being proud; help me to look at no one as lower than myself for all people were made in Your image with a purpose.[38]

---

36 Romans 8:1-2
37 Romans 12:1-2
38 Romans 12:9-16

I choose to crucify my sinful nature because I belong to Christ. Holy Spirit, help me to live by You and stay in step with You. Help me to bear and savor the fruit of Your Spirit: love, joy, peace, patience, kindness, goodness, faithfulness, gentleness, and self-control.[39]

Lord, help me sow seeds of life in the Holy Spirit that I might reap eternal life. Let me never become weary in doing good so that in the right season I will be able to harvest what I have sown. Help me to do good and be respectful to others, especially those who are part of the family of believers.[40]

Holy Spirit, when I begin to waver, remind me that I am surrounded by a great cloud of witnesses, so I can throw off anything hindering me from running my race on the path to Your Kingdom. Help me to keep my eyes fixed on Jesus, the author, and perfecter of my faith, who for the joy set before Him endured the cross, scorning its shame, and sat down at the right hand of the throne of God. Help me to consider Him who endured such opposition from sinful men, so that I will not grow weary and lose heart. In the midst of hardships remind me that You discipline those You love.[41]

---

39 Galatians 5:16-25
40 Galatians 6:7-10
41 Hebrews 12:1-7

Heavenly Father

I will trust in You with all my heart and lean not onto my own understanding. I will acknowledge You in all things and situations so that You can make my paths straight.[42] Help me to always seek wisdom and cherish its value above even money or success. Help me to reflect Your Spirit to the world as the Moon reflects the Sun to the Earth at night.

In Jesus' name, Amen.

---

42   Proverbs 3:6-7

7

Hurting and Broken

"I love the Lord, for he heard my voice;
   he heard my cry for mercy.
Because he turned his ear to me,
   I will call on him as long as I live.

The Lord is gracious and righteous;
   our God is full of compassion.
The Lord protects the unwary;
   when I was brought low, he saved me.
Return to your rest, my soul,
   for the Lord has been good to you."[43]

Lord, thank You for justifying me through faith, restoring my relationship with You. Thank You that I can stand before You in faith, rooted and grounded in grace. I rejoice in all situations because I know that You are good and You are

---

43   Psalm 116:1, 2, 5-7

with me. Thank You for this opportunity to suffer for Your name, knowing that perseverance, character, and hope are being developed within me. Thank You for giving me hope in You that never disappoints.[44]

Holy Spirit, help me understand that I live in a fallen world and I will gain scars as I walk through life. Remind me that each hurt, each failure, is only temporary as I move forward with you.

Jesus said, "I tell you, do not worry about your life, what you will eat; or about your body, what you will wear. Life is more than food, and the body more than clothes. Consider the ravens: They do not sow or reap, they have no storeroom or barn, yet God feeds them. And how much more valuable you are than birds! Who of you by worrying can add a single hour to his life? Since you cannot do this very little thing, why do you worry about the rest?"[45] Holy Spirit, teach me to have faith and not be anxious over things I cannot control. Help me to be like Shadrach, Meshach, and Abednego who put their trust in You even if it meant death. They learned, and I must also learn, that even if I die, I win in Christ because You have prepared a home for me in eternity.

---

44   Romans 5:1-5
45   Luke 12:22-26

Even in the midst of this situation, I choose to rejoice in You, Lord. I know that You are near to me, so I choose to give my worries and fears over to you. I am grateful for Your constant presence and I ask that Your peace would guard my heart and mind in Christ Jesus.[46]

Holy Spirit, help me to be grateful for what I do have and to bring all things to You. Teach me that all trials build my relationship with You. Thank you that each situation is an opportunity to grow in my belief and faith. Give me the certainty in who You are so that I may stand boldly in Your presence, knowing that I am in Christ and You are in me.

Paul told us, "Praise to God the Father of compassion and the God of comfort, who comforts us in all our troubles so that we can comfort those in any trouble with the comfort we ourselves have received from God. For just as the sufferings of Christ flow over in our lives, so also through Christ our comfort overflows."[47] Holy Spirit, help me understand that true joy, true peace, and true comfort only come from a complete surrender to You and allowing You to work through me no matter what the circumstances may be.

Lord, have Your will in my life. Forgive me for times when I have complained about the situations I find myself in; I

---

46 Philippians 4:4-7
47 2 Corinthians 1:3-5

Heavenly Father

choose to surrender to You once again. Make me pure and blameless, that I might be set apart for Your glory.[48]

Thank You for choosing me as part of your family; fill me with compassion, kindness, humility, gentleness, and patience. Help me to forgive anyone who I am holding a grudge against because You have freely forgiven me. Fill me with Your love, that I may walk in unity with my fellow believers. And let gratitude fill my heart and overflow from me, that I might glorify You in all I say and do.[49]

I know the enemy lurks around like a roaring lion (1 Peter 5:8), so Holy Spirit, remind me of who I am when I hear his roaring lies. Comfort me with the truth of Your Word and remind me that I am more than a conqueror in Christ.[50] Lord, keep my attention focused on You and give me an eternal perspective as I face trials and tests. Help me to stay faithful no matter what is thrown my way.

Help me, above all, to stand in the knowledge I am loved by the One who suffered and died for my sins even though He was blameless. Help me to always remember with praise and joy in my heart. I am a warrior for Christ but my battle is against sin, against Satan, and against the evil that has come

---

48 Philippians 2:12-16
49 Colossians 3:12-16
50 Romans 8:37

into this world. It is not with other people who were made in God's image, who have free will as I do.

Lord, remind me of Your sacrifice and forgiveness daily. Help me to share Your forgiveness with everyone I meet. I pray that You would mold me into one of the stars that shine for You so that I may point others back to You.

In Jesus' name, Amen.

8

God's Protection

I live within the shadow of the Almighty, sheltered by my God who is Lord of lords, King of kings, the Alpha and Omega, the Great I Am and my Creator.

I declare that You, O Father, are my refuge, my secure and fortified place. I put my trust and faith in You with all my heart and all that I am. I believe and know that You, O Lord, guide my steps so that I do not fall into temptation or snares that the enemy has placed before me. Help me to guard my heart.

Heavenly Father, You have equipped me with spiritual armor to allow me to stand, and You have placed a hedge of protection around me. I no longer fear evil or the terror of the night because I know that my soul and salvation are in Your hands. Thank You that my name is written on the palm of Your hand.

I will face all troubles and trials because I know Your Holy Spirit stands with me, giving me encouragement and strength. Thousands may fall or fail, but I will serve You, Lord. Ten thousand may run next to me and give up, still, I will trust in my salvation from Jesus Christ. I know on the day of judgment I will hear, "Come, my good and faithful servant."[51]

Lord, help me to always testify to my salvation, be fully dedicated to walking in step with You, and live as a living sacrifice. Because of my faithfulness to You, I long for you to say about me, "Because he loves me, I will rescue him; I will make him great because he trusts in my name. When he calls on me, I will answer; I will be with him in trouble and rescue him and honor him. I will satisfy him with a full life and give him my salvation."[52]

In Jesus' precious and mighty name, Amen!

---

51 Matthew 25:21
52 Psalm 91:14-16 (TLB)

9
Adult Children

Heavenly Father, thank You that You gave me the responsibility to rear children. Thank You for allowing me to be a part of Your creation process. I am grateful for the lessons I learn of Your love by trying to emulate You by being a parent.

Holy Spirit, please put a hedge of protection around my family as You did for Job,[53] I know that even Satan has to gain Your permission to get through that hedge. Thank You that You empower me to discern spiritual matters through Your Spirit.[54] Give me supernatural insight as I communicate with my adult children as they navigate through life.

Guide me to pray earnestly and daily for my children. Fill me with wisdom so I know when to be silent and when to speak. Help me discern the direction of Your Spirit and share words

---

53 Job 1:10
54 1 Corinthians 2:10-16

of wisdom at the appropriate time. Give me divine insight so that I know when to help them and when I need to step back and allow You to lovingly discipline them.[55]

Remind me daily that this person, who was once a child under my instruction, is now an adult. Help me see them as such and give me strategies to love them as they are. Lord, give me seasoned advice in the proper way, at the proper time, that they might receive Your wisdom.

Finally, Lord, I want to model what Paul has written in Philippians 4. Holy Spirit, work in my life so that I may rejoice in You, that my gentleness is evident to all. Help me to not be anxious about anything, but in everything, by prayer and petition, with thanksgiving, present my requests to You. Lord, I ask for Your peace, which transcends all understanding, to guard my heart and mind in Christ Jesus. Help me focus on what is true, noble, right, pure, lovely, admirable, and what is excellent and praiseworthy. I want to put into practice all that You have taught me[56] so my children can learn from my actions and example.

Lord, teach me how to be a parent of an adult.

In Jesus' name, Amen.

---

55 Hebrews 12:6
56 Philippians 4:4-9

10

Family Discipleship

Heavenly Father, I praise You that You place people in families.[57] I praise You that I am part of Your family and have a part of Your kingdom. I am grateful that You desire to have a relationship with me; thank You for being my Father in the truest sense. I praise You for fearfully, uniquely, and wonderfully making me[58] who I am.

Holy Spirit, I petition You to continue to put the hedge around me to protect me from sin and evil. Thank You for the angels that You have encamped around me because I fear You. Thank You for delivering me out of every trouble.[59]

Please help me believe and have faith in how much You love me. Give me the faith to believe that You not only have

---

57   Psalm 68:6
58   Psalm 139:14
59   Psalm 34:7

forgiven my sins but that You long for a relationship with me. Help me sense Your presence all around and within me. Remind me of the strength of Your love that is no match for my imperfections and sins. Help me to learn to trust in You with all my heart and not rely on my own wisdom.

Thank You for the gift of children. Fill me with Your Spirit that I might be an example to them. Give me wisdom and discernment as I teach my children about who You are and share Your great love. Remind me daily of Your love and the sacrifice of Your one and only Son[60] that has restored my personal relationship with You. May the truth of Your love be the foundation upon which my family is built.

Help me shepherd my children as You shepherd me, always pointing them back to who You are. Teach my children to hear Your voice, as the sheep know their shepherd and won't follow another.[61] Give me a passion for Your Word and voice that I may model for my children how to measure all things against the Bible. Help us to be a family unit that honors You.

In Jesus' name, Amen.

---

60   John 3:16
61   John 10:4, 11

11

Walking in Love

I will love You, O Lord, my strength. You are my rock, my fortress, and my deliverer.[62] Lord, I love You, along with all the saints. Thank You that You preserve the faithful and draw near to the humble. Lord, strengthen my heart as I continue to hope in You.[63]

Holy Spirit, teach me how to love. Help me to understand 1 Corinthians 13 and make it a part of my daily life. Fill my heart with Your love so that each word I speak is dripping with love. I pray that my speech never becomes mere noise. Remind me that all of the faith in the world without love amounts to nothing. Reorient my priorities so that Your love is of the utmost importance, more than even doing good

---

62 Psalm 18:1-2
63 Psalm 31:23-24

deeds or living a comfortable life. Help me to see others as Your creation so that I can love them as You love them.

Holy Spirit teach me that love will always be ready to suffer for long periods of time. Christ, thank You for the example You have provided for me in Your Word. Help me to imitate You in all things; being kind to those around me, rejoicing in the truth, enduring, believing, and hoping in all things, just as You do.

Instruct my heart and mind to understand that love does not envy, show off, is not prideful, rude, or selfish. Fill me with Your love that does not get provoked, does not think on or with evil, and does not rejoice over sin or failures. God, thank You for your love that does not cast the first stone.[64]

Holy Spirit, give me a love through Christ which never fails. Help me to abide in faith, hope, and above all, in Your love, which is full of mercy and grace. As I abide in You and Your love, I pray that Your joy would remain in me and be full. Show me how to love my brothers and sisters in Christ just as You have loved me. Help me comprehend sacrificial love so I can better appreciate those who have laid down their lives so I can worship You.[65]

---

64 1 Corinthians 13
65 John 15:11-13

Heavenly Father

Lord, direct my heart further into Your love and the patience of Christ.[66]

In Jesus' name, Amen.

---

[66] 2 Thessalonians 3:5 (NKJV)

12
Living a Holy Life

Heavenly Father, in Heaven, You are worthy of all my praise—I join with all of the angels in praising Your holy name![67] Your name alone is exalted above all else. Your glory surpasses the Earth and Heaven.[68]

"Search me, God, and know my heart; test me and know my anxious thoughts. See if there is any offensive way in me, and lead me in the way everlasting."[69]

> Like David, I pray, "Create in me a pure heart, O God,
>   and renew a steadfast spirit within me.
> Do not cast me from your presence
>   or take your Holy Spirit from me.

---

67   Psalm 148:1-2
68   Psalm 148:13
69   Psalm 139:23-24

Heavenly Father

> Restore to me the joy of your salvation
> and grant me a willing spirit, to sustain me.
> Then I will teach transgressors your ways,
> so that sinners will turn back to you.
> Deliver me from the guilt of bloodshed, O God,
> you who are God my Savior,
> and my tongue will sing of your righteousness.
> Open my lips, Lord,
> and my mouth will declare your praise."[70]

Just like Daniel, help me to purpose in my heart not to defile myself with what the world has to offer.[71] "May these words of my mouth and this meditation of my heart be pleasing in your sight, Lord, my Rock, and my Redeemer."[72]

Lord, I cry out to You; make haste to me! Give ear to my voice when I cry out to You. Let my prayer be set before You as incense, the lifting up of my hands as the evening sacrifice. Set a guard, O Lord over my mouth; keep watch over the door of my lips. Do not incline my heart to any evil thing, to practice wicked works with men who work iniquity; and do not let me eat of their delicacies.[73]

---

70 Psalm 51:10-15
71 Daniel 1:8
72 Psalm 19:14
73 Psalm 141:1-4

God of our Lord Jesus Christ, my glorious Father, give me the Spirit of wisdom and revelation, so that I may know You better. Enlighten the eyes of my heart so that I may know the hope to which You have called me, the riches of Your glorious inheritances in the saints, and Your incomparably great power for us to believe. Sanctify me completely, God of Peace, so that my whole spirit, soul, and body may be presented blameless at the coming of the Lord Jesus Christ. Lord, you are faithful, and I believe you will accomplish what you started in me.[74]

And this I pray, that my love may abound still more and more in knowledge and all discernment, that I may approve the things that are excellent. Lord, Jesus Christ, fill me with sincere faith and the fruit of righteousness so that I may be found without offense to the praise and glory of Your name.[75]

Help me to rejoice always, and pray without ceasing, and in every situation in life give thanks; for this is You will for me. Lord, fill me with a love for Your Spirit and a passion for the things of You. Help me test all things, holding fast to what is good and abstaining from every form of evil.[76]

---

74 Philippians 1:6
75 Philippians 1:9-11
76 1 Thessalonians 5:16-22

Heavenly Father

Oh, that You would bless me indeed, and enlarge my territory, that Your hand would be with me, and that You would keep me from evil, that I may not cause pain.[77] Lord, You said, "Call to me and I will answer and show you great and mighty things which you do not know." I am calling to You, show these to me.[78]

Lord, thank You that I do not war according to the flesh. For the weapons of my warfare are not carnal but mighty in You for the pulling down of strongholds, casting down arguments and every high thing that exalts itself against the knowledge of You. Christ, I choose to bring every thought into captivity to the obedience of You.[79]

I hold fast the confession of my hope without wavering, because You, O Lord, are faithful.[80] Help me to please You by believing that You exist and that you reward those who earnestly seek You.[81]

Lord, I pray Your Word back to You for I seek to know and possess Your truth and wisdom.

In Jesus' name, Amen.

---

77   1 Chronicles 4:10
78   Jeremiah 33:3
79   1 Corinthians 10:3-6
80   Hebrews 10:23
81   Hebrews 11:6

13
Troubles and Suffering

"O Lord, how long shall I cry,
And You will not hear?
Even cry out to You, "Violence!"
And You will not save.
Why do You show me iniquity,
And cause *me* to see trouble?
For plundering and violence *are* before me;
There is strife, and contention arises.
Therefore the law is powerless,
And justice never goes forth.
For the wicked surround the righteous;
Therefore perverse judgment proceeds."[82]

---

82 Habakkuk 1:2-4 (NKJV)

Heavenly Father

Lord, thank You that You are near to me, even when it seems as though the wicked are prospering.[83] Even in the fiery trial, thank You that I can choose to rejoice in You. Your presence and glory are my joy, even when things look bleak. Though I may be physically suffering, I am grateful that Your Spirit lives within me and your glory rests upon me. Show me, O God, how I can glorify you in this season of trial and difficulty.[84]

I humble myself under Your mighty hand, that You may lift me up in due time. I cast all my anxiety on You because You care for me. I long to be self-controlled and alert. My enemy, the devil prowls around like a roaring lion looking for someone to devour. I resist him, standing firm in my faith.[85]

Lord, thank You for giving me everything I need for life and godliness. You have called me by Your own glory and goodness, inviting me to partake in Your great and precious promises. Because of You, I can participate in the divine, escaping the world and its evil desires.[86]

Holy Spirit, help me have faith even when life has been so terrible. When my mind begins to doubt, fill me with faith in

---

83 Psalm 10:1-5
84 1 Peter 4:12-16
85 1 Peter 5:6-9
86 2 Peter 1:3-4

You and belief in Your Word. Give me the strength to stand, even when it costs me dearly. Guide my heart, thoughts, and actions, that I may remain focused on the goal of Heaven and living in Your presence someday.

In Jesus' name, Amen.

14
Standing on God's Word

Heavenly Father, help me to be like David when he wrote Psalm 31:7, "I will be glad and rejoice in your love, for you saw my affliction and knew the anguish of my soul." Even in the midst of difficulties and anguish, remind my heart and soul of Your everlasting love.

You have shown me what You require: to do justice, love mercy, and walk humbly with You.[87] Help me to treasure Your Word and empower me to walk this out.

Lord, I choose to look to you and wait for Your salvation. I thank You that You hear me when I cry to You.[88] "The Lord is my portion," says my soul, "Therefore I hope in Him!" I hope and wait for Your salvation.[89]

---

87 Micah 6:8
88 Micah 7:7
89 Lamentations 3:24, 26

Heavenly Father, even when persecution comes, help me to stand firm in You. Immerse me in the truth of Your Word that I may grow in faith and wisdom. Thank You for the Bible, which You inspired and is living and active. Holy Spirit, teach, correct, and instruct me in righteousness so that I may be complete and thoroughly equipped for every good work you have planned for me.[90]

Help me to grow, learn, and apply all instruction from the shepherds You put over me that I may understand who You are and the path I need to walk to reach my final destination in eternity.

Heavenly Father, bless me as Moses blessed Aaron and the priests that came after him. I am one of your spokespeople to this generation, so help me live a life so that others can see You reflected in me. Lord, bless and keep me. Make Your face shine upon me and be gracious to me. Lord, turn Your face toward me and give me peace.[91]

In Jesus' mighty name, Amen.

---

90   2 Timothy 3:12-17
91   Numbers 6:24-26

15
The Body of Christ

Heavenly Father, I give thanks to You, Your Son Jesus Christ, and the Holy Spirit for the faithfulness of pastors and other leaders in the church who constantly seek You, and pray for each other. Thank You for their faith and good works that encourage and uplift the saints in our congregations. Bless them for their willingness to grow in wisdom, knowledge, and understanding of Your Word.

Give me a burden for them, so I never cease praying for them. Holy Spirit, be with pastors and leaders that they would walk in a manner worthy of You, Lord. Help them be pleasing to all, fruitful in every good work, and increasing in the knowledge of who You are. Strengthen them so they are able to endure everything with perseverance, patience, and joy. Remind them of who You are, that they may abound in thanks to You, Father. May Your light shine brightly through them to a very dark and sinful world.

I praise You for offering salvation and forgiveness so I could step out of the darkness and into the light of Your mercy. Thank You for the grace that sets me free from the burden of sin. I praise You for sending Your Son, Jesus, to live, teach, die, and be resurrected so that I could find life and a way back to You.

Christ, You are the head of the church, remind our pastors and leaders of this truth daily. Holy Spirit, give them wisdom to create opportunities for fellowship, growth, and accountability among all believers. Most of all, empower all of Your people to demonstrate to the world the love and hope that is found in You.

Help Your church to continually lead people to the cross for salvation, to the empty tomb for hope, and to the day of Pentecost for learning how to grow with the aid of the Holy Spirit. Remind Your people that we were once sinners who have been forgiven. Increase our wisdom so that we may show hospitality and love to those around us. Holy Spirit, convict the hearts of our neighbors and friends, that they might be welcomed into Your family.

Lord, You know the intent of people's hearts, so I entrust the judgment of others to You. Help me, love, as Christ has

Heavenly Father

demonstrated. Keep my eyes fixed on eternity as I walk through life. Give me the words to openly testify about who You are through my actions, my words, and my life.[92]

In Jesus' name, Amen.

---

92 Colossians 1:9-23

16
The Church

Dear Lord, help the church to grow and become good stewards. Help us to continually praise and worship You.

Jesus, You told Peter, "on this rock I will build My church, and the gates of Hades shall not prevail against it. And I will give you the keys of the kingdom of heaven, and whatever you bind on earth will be bound in heaven, and whatever you loose on earth will be loosed in heaven."[93] You also told Your disciples that, "where two or three are gathered together in My name, I am there in the midst of them."[94] Lord, be in the midst of the church. Help us to seek Your wisdom, will, and discern the paths You want us to travel. Keep Your church holy and give us the wisdom to steward Your Word and Your Spirit well.

---

93   Matthew 16:18-19 (NKJV)
94   Matthew 18:20 (NKJV)

Heavenly Father

Lord, help our leaders understand that they have been made overseers by the Holy Spirit to shepherd the church of God, which has been purchased with Christ's blood.[95] Remind them of the truth of this great responsibility and empower them to lead with integrity and humility.

Lord, remind Your people of the importance of honoring and recognizing the shepherds and leaders in Your church. I pray that we would be a peace who live lives of peace and focus on the greater good. Put a passion within Your people to rejoice always, pray without ceasing, and always give thanks. Lord, be with us, that we may do Your will. Purify and sanctify Your church, Lord that we may be blameless before You. I hope and trust in You because You are faithful to finish what You began.[96]

Thank You for being our God and allowing us to be Your church.

In Jesus' name, Amen

---

95 Acts 20:28
96 1 Thessalonians 5:12-13, 15-23

17
School Districts

Heavenly Father, I praise You for the opportunity to enter Your throne room and petition You on behalf of schools. I have learned from Your Word to value wisdom and to teach the young so that when they are older they will not stray. I praise You that when I pray in unity with others, with faith even as small as a mustard seed, that You can do the impossible.

Please place a hedge of protection around schools. I ask that You would guard the buildings, the staff, the students, and all others who help these schools to run. I pray for safe transportation to and from school, whether students are walking, driving, or riding the bus. Fill each child with nourishment so their bodies, that You created, would grow properly and be ready to learn.

Your Word says, in Proverbs 2:3-6, "and if you call out for insight and cry aloud for understanding, and if you look for it as for silver and search for it as for hidden treasure, then you will understand the fear of the Lord and find the knowledge of God. For the Lord gives wisdom, and from his mouth come knowledge and understanding." I pray that all children, pre-teens, and teenagers who go to schools would hunger for insight and understanding. Give them a passion for studying and learning, so they can become well-prepared and mature adults. Father, help me be an example of love, grace, and integrity before them. Help me walk humbly and honestly, so they can be reminded that we learn from our failures too.

Heavenly Father, I come before You on behalf of all the teachers. Help them to develop the fruit of the Spirit by learning joy in what they do. Fill them with a supernatural love for all those who walk through their doors. Give them divine patience before their class. May they lead with kindness and live a life of humility before all people. Help teachers be a positive example in the lives of their students as they invest in and accept them no matter their faults and failures. Give strength and perseverance to all of the teachers so that they do not become cynical. Renew their minds so they can come to school fresh and ready to teach each day.

Lord, remind parents that learning does not stop at the school doors but also happens at home. Help parents learn to be role models and teachers also. Give parents the unswerving belief in their children and wisdom in how to properly correct them. May their homes be places where families flourish in knowledge, understanding, and discernment. Draw the parents to the church for rejuvenation, salvation, and support.

Help churches in this community provide support for parents, teens, and children. Holy Spirit, move in my community that we might be an example of the Kingdom of God to all. Teach each child, parent, teacher, and principal to put on the armor of God daily, so they might be prepared for all the negativity, hurt, and sin thrown their way.

Lord, thank You for calling Your church Your chosen people, holy and dearly loved. Show Your people how to speak, act, and live in a way that glorifies You. Whether in the classroom, the home, on the bus, or anywhere else, instruct Your chosen people how to live for You every day, with joy, peace, and gratitude.[97]

Amen.

---

97 Colossians 3:12-17

18
Pursuing Wisdom

Heavenly Father, I praise You for giving me a mind that is capable of reasoning and thought. I praise You for fearfully and wonderfully making me in Your image. I am grateful that You created me with a purpose and knew me before I was conceived in the womb. I also praise You for Your Word that I can seek and receive wisdom to see the world through Your eyes and with Your heart.

James wrote that, if anyone lacks wisdom, he should ask God, who gives generously to all without finding fault, and it will be given to him.[98] I come to You today seeking this wisdom. Help me take the first steps in wisdom by believing, "All scripture is given by inspiration of God, and is profitable for doctrine, for reproof, for correction, for instruction in

---

98   James 1:5 (NKJV)

righteousness, that the man of God may be complete, thoroughly equipped for every good work."[99]

Help me to trust in You with all my heart and lean not onto my own understanding. In all my ways I choose to acknowledge You, knowing that You will make my paths straight.[100]

Heavenly Father, help me seek after wisdom as if it was the most precious jewel to be found. Help me to learn to forgive, love, and serve others with a heart grounded in Your word, Your example, and Your sacrifice. Help me see all people as made in Your image with a purpose, remind me that they are all potential brothers and sisters in Christ.

Empower me to demonstrate Your love daily by pleasing my neighbor for his good, leading to edification. For even Christ did not please Himself; but as it is written, "The reproaches of those who reproached You fell on Me." For whatever things were written before were written for my learning, that I, through the patience and comfort of the Scriptures might have hope. Now may the God of patience and comfort grant me to be like-minded toward others, according to Christ Jesus, that I may with one mind and one mouth glorify the God and Father of our Lord Jesus Christ.[101]

---

99 2 Timothy 3:16-17 (NKJV)
100 Proverbs 3:5-6
101 Romans 15:2-6

Heavenly Father

Heavenly Father, Christ taught that if we ask it would be given to us.[102] I come to You seeking wisdom so that I can grow and mature into a person after Your own heart. Help me to learn to walk the path before me with an understanding that will lead others to You. Teach me to love obedience and see it as my strength and joy as I pursue the purpose You created me for.

Therefore, help me to be steadfast, immovable, always abounding in the work of the Lord, knowing that my labor is not in vain. Help me to watch, stand fast in the faith, be brave, and be strong. Let all that I do be done with love.[103]

In Jesus' name, Amen.

---

102 Matthew 7:7
103 1 Corinthians 15:58, 16:13

19
Joy in the Face of Trials

Heavenly Father, I know from the Bible that I should seek You at all times, but especially when I am brought so low that I feel I can no longer move forward or live any longer. Thank You for being a God who allows me to have a personal relationship that allows me to vent, rage, and complain, as well as praise and love. Help me to listen to You with my heart, mind, and soul and cling onto faith in You, when it seems that all else has fallen away.

> Help me to be like David who wrote,
> "How long, Lord? Will you forget me forever?
> How long will you hide your face from me?
> How long must I wrestle with my thoughts
>   and day after day have sorrow in my heart?
> How long will my enemy triumph over me?

> Look on me and answer, Lord my God.
>> Give light to my eyes, or I will sleep in death,
>> and my enemy will say, "I have overcome him,"
>>> and my foes will rejoice when I fall.
>
> But I trust in your unfailing love;
>> my heart rejoices in your salvation.
> I will sing the Lord's praise,
>> for he has been good to me."[104]

Help me to trust You enough to question as Habakkuk did in his writing, "O Lord, how long shall I cry, and You will not hear? Or cry to You, 'Violence!' and You will not save? Why do You make me see wickedness, and cause me to see trouble? Plundering and violence are before me; strife and contention arise. Therefore the law is powerless, and justice never goes forth. For the wicked surround the righteous; therefore injustice proceeds."[105]

Teach me to listen, learn, and understand as Paul did when he wrote in 1 Corinthians 2:11-16, "For who knows a person's thoughts except their own spirit within them? In the same way, no one knows the thoughts of God except the Spirit of God. What we have received is not the spirit of the world, but the Spirit who is from God, so that we may understand

---

104 Psalm 13
105 Habakkuk 1:2-4

what God has freely given us. This is what we speak, not in words taught us by human wisdom but in words taught by the Spirit, explaining spiritual realities with Spirit-taught words. The person without the Spirit does not accept the things that come from the Spirit of God but considers them foolishness, and cannot understand them because they are discerned only through the Spirit. The person with the Spirit makes judgments about all things, but such a person is not subject to merely human judgments, for,

"Who has known the mind of the Lord
 so as to instruct him?"

But we have the mind of Christ."

Father, I choose to come to You with all my burdens to accept the rest that Christ promised. Lord, I take your yoke and teaching. I choose to learn from You, accepting Your gentle and humble way of life. Thank You for providing the rest for my weary soul.[106]

In the midst of this trial, help me to count even this situation as pure joy, as James encourages. Lord, thank You for this moment of testing so that my faith can be made more perfect in You.[107]

---

106   Matthew 11:28-29
107   James 1:2-4

Lord, I choose to cling to the words written in the book of Hebrews, "Do you see what we've got? An unshakable kingdom! And do you see how thankful we must be? Not only thankful but brimming with worship, deeply reverent, before God. For God is not an indifferent bystander. He's actively cleaning house, torching all that needs to burn, and he won't quit until it's all cleansed. God himself is Fire!"[108]

God, thank you for this promise, "Never will I leave you; never will I forsake you."[109]

May my life's testimony be the words of David in Psalm 19, "May these words of my mouth and this meditation of my heart be pleasing in your sight, Lord, my Rock and my Redeemer."[110]

In Jesus' name, Amen.

---

[108] Hebrews 12:28-29 (The Message)
[109] Hebrews 13:5
[110] Psalm 19:14

20
Obedience to God

Heavenly Father, strengthen me with power through Your Spirit in my inner being so that Christ may dwell in my heart through faith. Root and establish me in Your love, so that I might understand the width, length, height, and depth of Your love for me. You are able to do immeasurably more than I can ask or imagine—be glorified in me, Your church, and throughout all generations.[111]

Holy Spirit, help me to daily offer my body as a living sacrifice, holy and pleasing to You—this is my spiritual act of worship. Help me to not conform any longer to the pattern of this world, but be transformed by the renewing of my mind. Then I will be able to test and approve what Your will is— Your good, pleasing and perfect will.[112] Help me to believe in

---

111 Ephesians 3:14-21
112 Romans 12:1-2

Heavenly Father

You and do the work that You did on the earth. Give me Your desires so that I may glorify Your name in all I say and do.[113]

Lord, teach me to be steadfast, immovable, and always abounding in the work of the Lord, knowing that my labor is not in vain.[114] Encourage me to watch, stand fast in the faith, be brave, and be strong. Let all that I do be done with love.[115]

Finally, sanctify my heart, and so I will always be ready to give a defense to everyone who asks me for the reason for the hope that is in me. Fill me with the meekness of Christ, the fear of You, and a good conscience that even when others speak out against me and my good conduct, I will not be afraid.[116]

I pray that my love may abound more and more. Lord, give me knowledge, depth, and insight into Your Word that I might be able to discern what is best. Purify and fill me with the fruit of righteousness that comes through Jesus Christ—to Your endless glory and praise.[117]

In Jesus' name, Amen.

---

113 John 14:12-14
114 1 Corinthians 15:58
115 1 Corinthians 16:13
116 1 Peter 3:15-16
117 Philippians 1:9-11

21
Producing Good Fruit

Lord, I praise You. I praise Your holy name because You created me and saved me. I join with all of the heavens and all of creation in glorifying You.[118]

Holy Spirit, help me live by Your direction so that I can resist the desires of my sinful nature. Help me to produce the fruit of Your Spirit in my life.

Teach me to have a love that is patient and kind to others. Help me to not envy, boast, or have pride in my heart. Keep me from being rude and self-seeking; help me to be slow and not easily angered. Help me to not keep any record of wrongs done against me. Continue to reveal truth to me, so that I will rejoice in it, instead of delighting in evil. Teach me to always

---
118   Psalm 148:1-6

trust, hope, and persevere in demonstrating my love to You and others.[119]

Holy Spirit, help me to become a child of the Father in Heaven by showing love to my enemies and praying for those who persecute me.[120] Remind me daily that in all things, I am more than a conqueror through Christ who loves me. Help me to be convinced that neither death nor life, neither angels nor demons, neither the present nor the future, nor any powers, neither height nor depth, nor anything else in all creation, will be able to separate me from the love of God that is in Christ Jesus.[121]

Show me, like You showed Nehemiah, that the joy of the Lord is my strength.[122] Fill me with Your wisdom and peace that I might abound in joy and honor You. Help me to be a wise heir so I bring joy to my Father.[123] Help me to have joy because I promote peace.[124] Help me to ask as Christ told us to so that my joy may be complete.[125] Allow me to build Your kingdom into my heart so that I have righteousness, peace, and joy in the Holy Spirit because anyone who serves You in

---

119 1 Corinthians 13:4-7
120 Matthew 5:44
121 Romans 8:37-39
122 Nehemiah 8:10
123 Proverbs 10:1
124 Proverbs 12:20
125 John 16:24

this way is pleasing to God and approved by men.[126] Help me to always pray with joy as Paul did.[127] Help me to be joyful always; pray continually; and give thanks in all circumstances, for this is Your will for me.[128]

Lord, You are the Lord of peace, give peace to me at all times and in every way so I can reflect Your love.[129] Help me to seek harmony with others and pursue peace everywhere I go[130]. Christ Jesus, guard my heart and mind with Your peace that transcends all understanding.[131] Lord, grant peace to my borders as David talks about in Psalms[132]. Help me to promote peace so that I have joy.[133] Holy Spirit, lead me on the path of peace[134] and help me to be a peacemaker.[135]

Lord, help me to demonstrate patience towards others even when I do not feel like it instead of displaying quick-tempered folly.[136] Help me to warn those who are idle, encourage the

---

126 Romans 14:17-18
127 Philippians 1:4
128 1 Thessalonians 5:16
129 2 Thessalonians 3:16
130 1 Peter 3:8-12
131 Philippians 4:7
132 Psalm 147:14
133 Proverbs 12:20
134 Luke 1:79
135 Matthew 5:9
136 Proverbs 14:29

Heavenly Father

timid, help the weak, and be patient with everyone.[137] Give me the strength to be patient and stand firm without grumbling or judging.[138]

Holy Spirit, clothe me in kindness so that I reflect Your love and grace to those around me. give me kindness so I can continue in kindness.[139] Help me to be clothed in kindness as I represent Your chosen people.[140] Help me to add to my faith kindness so I can be productive in my knowledge of You.[141] Help me to learn to be kind so that I reflect Your love and grace.

Lord, help me to turn from evil and do good; seek peace and pursue it.[142] Help me to conduct my affairs with justice, and be generous so that good will come to me.[143] And when it is in my power to act, help me not to withhold good from those who deserve it.[144] Help me to never seek evil, but always seek good, so I can find it.[145] Help me to plan what is good so that I find love and faithfulness.[146] Make me into good soil so that

---

137   1 Thessalonians 5:14
138   James 5:8-9
139   Romans 11:22
140   Colossians 3:12
141   2 Peter 1:7
142   Psalm 34:14
143   Psalm 112:5
144   Proverbs 3:27
145   Proverbs 11:27
146   Proverbs 14:22

whatever seeds You plant in me will grow and produce fruit to help others learn of Your kingdom.[147]

Holy Spirit, appoint Your love and faithfulness to protect and surround me.[148] Help me reflect on Your abounding love and faithfulness[149] to all generations.[150] I long to be known as one who is faithful to You and Your principles.

Lord, let my gentleness be evident to all.[151] Clothe me in Your gentleness[152] that I might always be ready to answer everyone who asks for the reason for my hope.[153]

Holy Spirit, add to my faith, self-control so I can be productive in my faith and knowledge of Jesus Christ. (2Peter 1:6) Thank You for Your grace that teaches me to live a self-controlled and godly life as I continue to hope in You. (Titus 2:11-13) Fill me with self-control and spiritual awareness that I will stand firm and resist the devil when he roars at me. (1Peter 5:8&9)

---

147 Matthew 13:8
148 Psalm 61:7
149 Psalm 86:15
150 Psalm 89:1
151 Philippians 4:5
152 Colossians 3:12
153 1 Peter 3:15-16

Heavenly Father

Lord, fill me with Your Spirit, that I may bear Your fruit throughout my life. Help me continually grow more fruit as long as I live so that I can glorify You.

In Jesus' Name, Amen.

22
An Athlete's Prayer

Heavenly Father, thank You for giving me the talents and abilities to compete as an athlete. I'm grateful for this privilege to learn about struggle and competition while demonstrating respect and loyalty. Help me to glorify You in this game, as I give all that I have. Thank You for my teammates who I'm learning to trust as I'm also learning to trust You.

Lord, You told us that with God all things are possible.[154] Help me to believe that through You, my team and I can accomplish our goals. I know You have made me for this time and place, so help me to represent You as I become the best possible player and teammate I can be. Help me protect and fight for them with all that I have on the field, court, diamond, or ice and to leave the game knowing I could give no

---

154 Matthew 19:26

Heavenly Father

more than I did. Help me have faith in my ability and those around me and to leave the rest in your hands. May You be honored in me as I do my best.

In Jesus' name, Amen.

23
Exercising your Body

Dear Lord, I praise You and Your name. You have searched and known me, and still love me.[155] I will praise You, for I am fearfully and wonderfully made. My soul knows the marvelous nature of Your works.[156] May my words and thoughts be acceptable in Your sight, O Lord, my strength and my Redeemer.[157]

I present my body a living sacrifice, holy, acceptable to You, which is my reasonable service. Help me not to be like this world, but be transformed by the renewing of my mind, that I may prove Your good, acceptable, and perfect will.[158]

---

155 Psalm 139:1
156 Psalm 139:14
157 Psalm 19:14
158 Romans 12:1-2

Heavenly Father

Remind me that I am Yours and that You are greater than he who is in the world.[159]

Lord, You give power to the weak[160] and because of Your strength, I can do all things.[161] Thank You that in all things I am more than a conqueror through Christ who loves me.[162]

> I choose to echo the psalmist, David, when he wrote
> "But I will sing of your strength,
> in the morning I will sing of your love;
> for you are my fortress,
> my refuge in times of trouble.
>
> You are my strength, I sing praise to you;
> you, God, are my fortress,
> my God on whom I can rely."[163]

Thank You for making me who I am. Help me trust that You are faithful to help me grow and be strong in body and in the truth of Your Word. Help me be a temple that praises You and brings others to You.

In Jesus' powerful and wonderful name. Amen.

---

159   1 John 4:4
160   Isaiah 40:29
161   Philippians 4:13
162   Romans 8:37
163   Psalm 59:16-17

24
Handling Money

Heavenly Father, thank You for teaching me to be a good steward of all You give me. I'm grateful for the seasons of abundance, where You've taught me responsibility, and for the seasons of lack, where You have grown my faith.

Holy Spirit, help me to learn wisdom from Jesus' parable on the talents, recorded in Matthew 25. Fill my heart with generosity so that I will always be willing to invest what You've given me into growing Your Kingdom.

"Bring all the tithes into the storehouse, that there may be food in My house, and test Me now in this, says the Lord of Hosts, if I will not open for you the windows of heaven and pour out for you a blessing, that *there will* not *be room enough to receive it*."[164] Holy Spirit, help me to realize this promise of blessing does not mean money.

---

164   Malachi 3:10 (MEV)

Heavenly Father, teach my household to be wise with our finances so I can tithe, pay what I owe, and give when I can to be generous to others. Help me to give my money, time, talents, and encouragement. Teach me the joy of giving and remind me that it's more blessed to give than to receive.[165]

Heavenly Father, help me to be faithful in the small things so that when the time comes I will be ready to be faithful with bigger responsibilities. Fill my heart with joy, so that I may give cheerfully.[166] Give me wisdom so that I can glorify You in all my finances.

Help me to learn that Your wisdom is more valuable than gold, and Your spiritual discernment is more valuable than rubies. Give me an eternal perspective so that I store up my treasures in Heaven so that my possessions don't become an anchor around my heart.[167] I long for You to be first in all I do, all I receive, and all that I am given responsibility for.

In Jesus' name, Amen.

---

165   Acts 20:35
166   2 Corinthians 9:7
167   Matthew 6:19-21

25
Physical and Mental Health

Heavenly Father, I praise You for Your Word and for all the wisdom you give me. Thank You for the wisdom that you have given doctors to improve people's lives and for being the ultimate Healer.

Holy Spirit, continue to remind me that You created me in my mother's womb with a purpose. Help me learn what that purpose is and fulfill it. Thank You for designing me so specifically for Your glory; when I begin to doubt, remind me that You created me to honor You, not myself or anyone else. Lord, You know each one of my days, help me to savor today and fill it with prayer, praise, and service to You.[168]

---

168   Psalm 139:13-16

Heavenly Father

James wrote, "Is anyone among you suffering? Let him pray. Is anyone cheerful? Let him sing psalms. Is anyone among you sick? Let him call for the elders of the church, and let them pray over him, anointing him with oil in the name of the Lord. And the prayer of faith will save the sick, and the Lord will raise him up. And if he has committed sins, he will be forgiven."[169] "Therefore confess your sins to each other and pray for each other so that you may be healed. The prayer of a righteous person is powerful and effective."[170]

Lord, no matter what I'm facing—sickness, disease, mental health issues, pains, broken bones, or anything else—remind me to always come to You for healing, guidance, and faith. Give me wisdom and revelation and lead me to the right people who can use the gifts You gave them to help me attempt to heal.

I will cast all my anxiety on You because I know You care for me. With Your help, I will be self-controlled and alert. I will resist my enemy, standing firm in my faith. I know that You will restore me and make me strong, firm, and steadfast.[171]

In Jesus' name, Amen.

---

169 James 5:13-15 (NKJV)
170 James 5:16
171 1 Peter 5:6-11

26
Leading People

Heavenly Father, I praise You for the gifts You've given me and the opportunities to use them. Thank You for Your Word and Christ's example in how to lead.

Holy Spirit, give me a passion for serving people that I may humbly lead as Christ did. You didn't consider Yourself too important to wash even the disciples' stinky feet; help me to maintain that same humble perspective.

Heavenly Father, help me to be meek like Moses, so I can fully lean on You as I lead. Help me learn from the wisdom of the people around me. Give me the courage and insight to delegate responsibilities to others. Fill me with joy and encouragement that I can share with those I'm leading.

Like Caleb, give me a boldness to take you at Your Word and stand firmly on Your promises. Help me to see the potential in others and give me a conquering mindset, regardless of the circumstances around me.

Thank You for the courage You have placed inside of me to do Your will. Like you did for Joshua, remind me of Your presence, Your guidance, and Your discernment as I lead.

Like Gideon, give me the spiritual eyes to see there's more than enough with You, even when resources look scarce.

When there is a vacancy, fill me with the faith of the apostles, who valued character and Your Spirit over all else.

Lord, fill me with your perspective; that I would see everyone I lead as made in Your image. That I would love them as You have loved them. Remind me to never see myself as higher than anyone else.

Empower me to fulfill what Paul wrote in Romans 15, "Let each of us please *his* neighbor for *his* good, leading to edification. For even Christ did not please Himself, but as it is written, "The reproaches of those who reproached You fell on Me." For whatever things were written before were written for our learning, that we through the patience and comfort of the Scriptures might have hope. Now may the God of patience and comfort grant you to be like-minded toward one another, according to Christ Jesus, that you may with one mind *and* one mouth glorify the God and Father of our Lord Jesus Christ."[172]

Help me to be a leader who sees with Your eyes, listens with Your ears, and discerns with Your wisdom so that I can glorify You as I build others up.

In Jesus' name, Amen.

---

[172] Romans 15:2-6 (NKJV)

APPENDIX
Scriptures from footnotes

Following Jesus

Psalm 19:14 "May these words of my mouth and this meditation of my heart be pleasing in your sight, Lord, my Rock and my Redeemer."

Proverbs 2:1-6 "My son, if you accept my words
    and store up my commands within you,
turning your ear to wisdom
    and applying your heart to understanding—
indeed, if you call out for insight
    and cry aloud for understanding,
and if you look for it as for silver
    and search for it as for hidden treasure,
then you will understand the fear of the Lord
    and find the knowledge of God.
For the Lord gives wisdom;
    from his mouth come knowledge and understanding."

Romans 12:2 "Do not conform to the pattern of this world, but be transformed by the renewing of your mind. Then you will be able to test and approve what God's will is—his good, pleasing and perfect will."

James 1:22 "Do not merely listen to the word, and so deceive yourselves. Do what it says."

Hebrews 11:6 "And without faith it is impossible to please God, because anyone who comes to him must believe that he exists and that he rewards those who earnestly seek him."

Proverbs 3:5-6 "Trust in the Lord with all your heart
    and lean not on your own understanding;
in all your ways submit to him,
    and he will make your paths straight."

Romans 12:15 "Rejoice with those who rejoice; mourn with those who mourn."

Using the Lord's Prayer as a Guide

Matthew 6:9-13 "This, then, is how you should pray:

"Our Father in heaven,
hallowed be your name,
your kingdom come,
your will be done,

> on earth as it is in heaven.
> Give us today our daily bread.
> And forgive us our debts,
> > as we also have forgiven our debtors.
> And lead us not into temptation,
> > but deliver us from the evil one"

Jude 24-25 (NLT) "Now all glory to God, who is able to keep you from falling away and will bring you with great joy into his glorious presence without a single fault. All glory to him who alone is God, our Savior through Jesus Christ our Lord. All glory, majesty, power, and authority are his before all time, and in the present, and beyond all time! Amen."

Isaiah 25:1 "Lord, you are my God;
> I will exalt you and praise your name,
for in perfect faithfulness
> you have done wonderful things,
> > things planned long ago."

Romans 12:1-2 "Therefore, I urge you, brothers and sisters, in view of God's mercy, to offer your bodies as a living sacrifice, holy and pleasing to God—this is your true and proper worship. Do not conform to the pattern of this world, but be transformed by the renewing of your mind. Then you will be able to test and approve what God's will is—his good, pleasing and perfect will."

Mark 16:15-18 "He said to them, "Go into all the world and preach the gospel to all creation. Whoever believes and is baptized will be saved, but whoever does not believe will be condemned. And these signs will accompany those who believe: In my name they will drive out demons; they will speak in new tongues; they will pick up snakes with their hands; and when they drink deadly poison, it will not hurt them at all; they will place their hands on sick people, and they will get well."

Mark 16:20 "Then the disciples went out and preached everywhere, and the Lord worked with them and confirmed his word by the signs that accompanied it."

Luke 12:22-31 "Then Jesus said to his disciples: "Therefore I tell you, do not worry about your life, what you will eat; or about your body, what you will wear. For life is more than food, and the body more than clothes. Consider the ravens: They do not sow or reap, they have no storeroom or barn; yet God feeds them. And how much more valuable you are than birds! Who of you by worrying can add a single hour to your life? Since you cannot do this very little thing, why do you worry about the rest?

Consider how the wild flowers grow. They do not labor or spin. Yet I tell you, not even Solomon in all his splendor was dressed like one of these. If that is how God clothes the grass of the field, which is here today, and tomorrow is thrown into the fire, how much more will he clothe you—you of little faith! And do not set your heart on what you will eat or drink; do not worry about it. For the pagan world runs after all such things, and your Father knows that you need them. But seek his kingdom, and these things will be given to you as well."

Philippians 4:4-7 "Rejoice in the Lord always. I will say it again: Rejoice! Let your gentleness be evident to all. The Lord is near. Do not be anxious about anything, but in every situation, by prayer and petition, with thanksgiving, present your requests to God. And the peace of God, which transcends all understanding, will guard your hearts and your minds in Christ Jesus."

John 20:21-23 "Again Jesus said, "Peace be with you! As the Father has sent me, I am sending you." And with that he breathed on them and said, "Receive the Holy Spirit. If you forgive anyone's sins, their sins are forgiven; if you do not forgive them, they are not forgiven."

Romans 5:1-5 "Therefore, since we have been justified through faith, we have peace with God through our Lord Jesus Christ, through whom we have gained access by faith into this grace in which we now stand. And we boast in the hope of the glory of God. Not only so, but we also glory in our sufferings, because we know that suffering produces perseverance; perseverance, character; and character, hope. And hope does not put us to shame, because God's love has been poured out into our hearts through the Holy Spirit, who has been given to us."

2 Thessalonians 3:5 "May the Lord direct your hearts into God's love and Christ's perseverance."

Learning to Forgive

Mark 11:25 "And when you stand praying, if you hold anything against anyone, forgive them, so that your Father in heaven may forgive you your sins."

2 Corinthians 2:11 "in order that Satan might not outwit us. For we are not unaware of his schemes."

1 Peter 4:7-11 "The end of all things is near. Therefore be alert and of sober mind so that you may pray. Above all, love each other deeply, because love covers over a multitude of sins. Offer hospitality to one another without grumbling. Each of you should use whatever gift you have received to serve others, as faithful stewards of God's grace in its various forms. If anyone speaks, they should do so as one who speaks the very words of God. If anyone serves, they should do so with the strength God provides, so that in all things God may be praised through Jesus Christ. To him be the glory and the power for ever and ever. Amen."

Philippians 2:12-13 "Therefore, my dear friends, as you have always obeyed—not only in my presence, but now much more in my absence—continue to work out your salvation with fear and trembling, for it is God who works in you to will and to act in order to fulfill his good purpose."

2 Thessalonians 3:5 "May the Lord direct your hearts into God's love and Christ's perseverance."

Growing in Faith

Psalm 18:1-2 "I love you, Lord, my strength.
The Lord is my rock, my fortress and my deliverer;
    my God is my rock, in whom I take refuge,
    my shield and the horn of my salvation, my stronghold."

Mark 11:23 "Truly I tell you, if anyone says to this mountain, 'Go, throw yourself into the sea,' and does not doubt in their heart but believes that what they say will happen, it will be done for them."

Hebrews 11:6 "And without faith it is impossible to please God, because anyone who comes to him must believe that he exists and that he rewards those who earnestly seek him."

Matthew 21:22 "If you believe, you will receive whatever you ask for in prayer."

Mark 16:17-18 "And these signs will accompany those who believe: In my name they will drive out demons; they will speak in new tongues; they will pick up snakes with their hands; and when they drink deadly poison, it will not hurt them at all; they will place their hands on sick people, and they will get well."

Psalm 116:2 "Because he turned his ear to me,
 I will call on him as long as I live."

1 Peter 3:12 "For the eyes of the Lord are on the righteous
 and his ears are attentive to their prayer,
but the face of the Lord is against those who do evil."

Galatians 5:22-23 "But the fruit of the Spirit is love, joy, peace, forbearance, kindness, goodness, faithfulness, gentleness and self-control. Against such things there is no law."

Galatians 5:25 "Since we live by the Spirit, let us keep in step with the Spirit."

Wearing the Armor of God

Psalm 145:1-5 "I will exalt you, my God the King;
 I will praise your name for ever and ever.
Every day I will praise you
 and extol your name for ever and ever.
Great is the Lord and most worthy of praise;

> his greatness no one can fathom.
> One generation commends your works to another;
> > they tell of your mighty acts.
> They speak of the glorious splendor of your majesty—
> > and I will meditate on your wonderful works."

Job 1:10 "Have you not put a hedge around him and his household and everything he has? You have blessed the work of his hands, so that his flocks and herds are spread throughout the land."

Ephesians 6:10-20 "Finally, be strong in the Lord and in his mighty power. Put on the full armor of God, so that you can take your stand against the devil's schemes. For our struggle is not against flesh and blood, but against the rulers, against the authorities, against the powers of this dark world and against the spiritual forces of evil in the heavenly realms. Therefore put on the full armor of God, so that when the day of evil comes, you may be able to stand your ground, and after you have done everything, to stand. Stand firm then, with the belt of truth buckled around your waist, with the breastplate of righteousness in place, and with your feet fitted with the readiness that comes from the gospel of peace. In addition to all this, take up the shield of faith, with which you can extinguish all the flaming arrows of the evil one. Take the helmet of salvation and the sword of the Spirit, which is the word of God.

And pray in the Spirit on all occasions with all kinds of prayers and requests. With this in mind, be alert and always keep on praying for all the Lord's people. Pray also for me, that whenever I speak, words may be given me so that I will fearlessly make known the mystery of the gospel, for which I am an ambassador in chains. Pray that I may declare it fearlessly, as I should."

2 Corinthians 5:7 "For we live by faith, not by sight."

2 Corinthians 10:3-5 "For though we live in the world, we do not wage war as the world does. The weapons we fight with are not the weapons of the world. On the contrary, they have divine power to demolish strongholds. We demolish arguments and every pretension that sets itself up against the knowledge of God, and we take captive every thought to make it obedient to Christ."

2 Timothy 1:7 "For the Spirit God gave us does not make us timid, but gives us power, love and self-discipline."

2 Timothy 3:16-17 "All Scripture is God-breathed and is useful for teaching, rebuking, correcting and training in righteousness, so that the servant of God may be thoroughly equipped for every good work."

Psalm 19:14 "May these words of my mouth and this
   meditation of my heart

be pleasing in your sight,
Lord, my Rock and my Redeemer."

Mind and Spirit

Psalm 33:1-5 "Sing joyfully to the Lord, you righteous;
it is fitting for the upright to praise him.
Praise the Lord with the harp;
make music to him on the ten-stringed lyre.
Sing to him a new song;
play skillfully, and shout for joy.
For the word of the Lord is right and true;
he is faithful in all he does.
The Lord loves righteousness and justice;
the earth is full of his unfailing love."

Romans 8:1-2 "Therefore, there is now no condemnation for those who are in Christ Jesus, because through Christ Jesus the law of the Spirit who gives life has set you free from the law of sin and death."

Romans 12:1-2 "Therefore, I urge you, brothers and sisters, in view of God's mercy, to offer your bodies as a living sacrifice, holy and pleasing to God—this is your true and proper worship. Do not conform to the pattern of this world, but be transformed by the renewing of your mind. Then you will be able to test and approve what God's will is—his good, pleasing and perfect will."

Romans 12:9-16 "Love must be sincere. Hate what is evil; cling to what is good. Be devoted to one another in love. Honor one another above yourselves. Never be lacking in zeal, but keep your spiritual fervor, serving the Lord. Be joyful in hope, patient in affliction, faithful in prayer. Share with the Lord's people who are in need. Practice hospitality.

Bless those who persecute you; bless and do not curse. Rejoice with those who rejoice; mourn with those who mourn. Live in harmony with one another. Do not be proud, but be willing to associate with people of low position. Do not be conceited."

Galatians 5:16-25 "So I say, walk by the Spirit, and you will not gratify the desires of the flesh. For the flesh desires what is contrary to the Spirit, and the Spirit what is contrary to the flesh. They are in conflict with each other, so that you are not to do whatever you want. But if you are led by the Spirit, you are not under the law.

The acts of the flesh are obvious: sexual immorality, impurity and debauchery; idolatry and witchcraft; hatred, discord, jealousy, fits of rage, selfish ambition, dissensions, factions and envy; drunkenness, orgies, and the like. I warn you, as I did before, that those who live like this will not inherit the kingdom of God.

But the fruit of the Spirit is love, joy, peace, forbearance, kindness, goodness, faithfulness, gentleness and self-control.

Against such things there is no law. Those who belong to Christ Jesus have crucified the flesh with its passions and desires. Since we live by the Spirit, let us keep in step with the Spirit."

Galatians 6:7-10 "Do not be deceived: God cannot be mocked. A man reaps what he sows. Whoever sows to please their flesh, from the flesh will reap destruction; whoever sows to please the Spirit, from the Spirit will reap eternal life. Let us not become weary in doing good, for at the proper time we will reap a harvest if we do not give up. Therefore, as we have opportunity, let us do good to all people, especially to those who belong to the family of believers."

Hebrews 12:1-7 "Therefore, since we are surrounded by such a great cloud of witnesses, let us throw off everything that hinders and the sin that so easily entangles. And let us run with perseverance the race marked out for us, fixing our eyes on Jesus, the pioneer and perfecter of faith. For the joy set before him he endured the cross, scorning its shame, and sat down at the right hand of the throne of God. Consider him who endured such opposition from sinners, so that you will not grow weary and lose heart.

In your struggle against sin, you have not yet resisted to the point of shedding your blood. And have you completely forgotten this word of encouragement that addresses you as a father addresses his son? It says,

"My son, do not make light of the Lord's discipline,
    and do not lose heart when he rebukes you,
because the Lord disciplines the one he loves,

and he chastens everyone he accepts as his son."

Endure hardship as discipline; God is treating you as his children. For what children are not disciplined by their father?"

Proverbs 3:6-7 "in all your ways submit to him,
    and he will make your paths straight.
Do not be wise in your own eyes;
    fear the Lord and shun evil."

Hurting and Broken

Psalm 116:1-2, 5-7 "I love the Lord, for he heard my voice;
    he heard my cry for mercy.
Because he turned his ear to me,
    I will call on him as long as I live.

"The Lord is gracious and righteous;
    our God is full of compassion.
The Lord protects the unwary;
    when I was brought low, he saved me.
Return to your rest, my soul,
    for the Lord has been good to you."

Heavenly Father

Romans 5:1-5 "Therefore, since we have been justified through faith, we have peace with God through our Lord Jesus Christ, through whom we have gained access by faith into this grace in which we now stand. And we boast in the hope of the glory of God. Not only so, but we also glory in our sufferings, because we know that suffering produces perseverance; perseverance, character; and character, hope. And hope does not put us to shame, because God's love has been poured out into our hearts through the Holy Spirit, who has been given to us."

Luke 12:22-26 "Then Jesus said to his disciples: "Therefore I tell you, do not worry about your life, what you will eat; or about your body, what you will wear. For life is more than food, and the body more than clothes. Consider the ravens: They do not sow or reap, they have no storeroom or barn; yet God feeds them. And how much more valuable you are than birds! Who of you by worrying can add a single hour to your life? Since you cannot do this very little thing, why do you worry about the rest?"

Philippians 4:4-7 "Rejoice in the Lord always. I will say it again: Rejoice! Let your gentleness be evident to all. The Lord is near. Do not be anxious about anything, but in every situation, by prayer and petition, with thanksgiving, present your requests to God. And the peace of God, which transcends all understanding, will guard your hearts and your minds in Christ Jesus."

2 Corinthians 1:3-5 "Praise be to the God and Father of our Lord Jesus Christ, the Father of compassion and the God of all comfort, who comforts us in all our troubles, so that we can comfort those in any trouble with the comfort we ourselves receive from God. For just as we share abundantly in the sufferings of Christ, so also our comfort abounds through Christ."

Philippians 2:12-16 "Therefore, my dear friends, as you have always obeyed—not only in my presence, but now much more in my absence—continue to work out your salvation with fear and trembling, for it is God who works in you to will and to act in order to fulfill his good purpose.

Do everything without grumbling or arguing, so that you may become blameless and pure, "children of God without fault in a warped and crooked generation." Then you will shine among them like stars in the sky as you hold firmly to the word of life. And then I will be able to boast on the day of Christ that I did not run or labor in vain."

Colossians 3:12-16 "Therefore, as God's chosen people, holy and dearly loved, clothe yourselves with compassion, kindness, humility, gentleness and patience. Bear with each other and forgive one another if any of you has a grievance against someone. Forgive as the Lord forgave you. And over all these virtues put on love, which binds them all together in perfect unity.

Let the peace of Christ rule in your hearts, since as members of one body you were called to peace. And be thankful. Let the message of Christ dwell among you richly as you teach and admonish one another with all wisdom through psalms, hymns, and songs from the Spirit, singing to God with gratitude in your hearts."

Romans 8:37 "No, in all these things we are more than conquerors through him who loved us."

God's Protection

Matthew 25:21 "His master replied, 'Well done, good and faithful servant! You have been faithful with a few things; I will put you in charge of many things. Come and share your master's happiness!'"

Psalm 91:14-16 (TLB) "For the Lord says, "Because he loves me, I will rescue him; I will make him great because he trusts in my name. When he calls on me, I will answer; I will be with him in trouble and rescue him and honor him. I will satisfy him with a full life and give him my salvation."

Adult Children

Job 1:10 "Have you not put a hedge around him and his household and everything he has? You have blessed the work of his hands, so that his flocks and herds are spread throughout the land."

1 Corinthians 2:10-16 "The Spirit searches all things, even the deep things of God. For who knows a person's thoughts except their own spirit within them? In the same way no one knows the thoughts of God except the Spirit of God. What we have received is not the spirit of the world, but the Spirit who is from God, so that we may understand what God has freely given us. This is what we speak, not in words taught us by human wisdom but in words taught by the Spirit, explaining spiritual realities with Spirit-taught words. The person without the Spirit does not accept the things that come from the Spirit of God but considers them foolishness, and cannot understand them because they are discerned only through the Spirit. The person with the Spirit makes judgments about all things, but such a person is not subject to merely human judgments, for,

"Who has known the mind of the Lord
    so as to instruct him?"
But we have the mind of Christ."

Hebrews 12:6 "because the Lord disciplines the one he loves, and he chastens everyone he accepts as his son."

Philippians 4:4-9 "Rejoice in the Lord always. I will say it again: Rejoice! Let your gentleness be evident to all. The Lord is near. Do not be anxious about anything, but in every situation, by prayer and petition, with thanksgiving, present your requests to God. And the peace of God, which transcends all understanding, will guard your hearts and your minds in Christ Jesus.

Finally, brothers and sisters, whatever is true, whatever is noble, whatever is right, whatever is pure, whatever is lovely, whatever is admirable—if anything is excellent or praiseworthy—think about such things. Whatever you have learned or received or heard from me, or seen in me—put it into practice. And the God of peace will be with you."

Family Discipleship

Psalm 68:6 "God sets the lonely in families,
    he leads out the prisoners with singing;
    but the rebellious live in a sun-scorched land."

Psalm 139:14 "I praise you because I am fearfully and
    wonderfully made;
    your works are wonderful,
    I know that full well."

Psalm 34:7 "The angel of the Lord encamps around
    those who fear him,
    and he delivers them."

John 3:16 "For God so loved the world that he gave his one and only Son, that whoever believes in him shall not perish but have eternal life."

John 10:4, 11 "When he has brought out all his own, he goes on ahead of them, and his sheep follow him because they know his voice... I am the good shepherd. The good shepherd lays down his life for the sheep."

Walking in Love

Psalm 18:1-2 "I love you, Lord, my strength.
The Lord is my rock, my fortress and my deliverer;
    my God is my rock, in whom I take refuge,
    my shield and the horn of my salvation, my stronghold."

Psalm 31:23-24 "Love the Lord, all his faithful people!
    The Lord preserves those who are true to him,
    but the proud he pays back in full.
Be strong and take heart,
    all you who hope in the Lord."

1 Corinthians 13 "If I speak in the tongues of men or of angels, but do not have love, I am only a resounding gong or a clanging cymbal. If I have the gift of prophecy and can fathom all mysteries and all knowledge, and if I have a faith that can move mountains, but do not have love, I am nothing. If I give all I possess to the poor and give over my body to hardship that I may boast, but do not have love, I gain nothing.

Love is patient, love is kind. It does not envy, it does not boast, it is not proud. It does not dishonor others, it is not self-seeking, it is not easily angered, it keeps no record of wrongs. Love does not delight in evil but rejoices with the truth. It always protects, always trusts, always hopes, always perseveres.

Love never fails. But where there are prophecies, they will cease; where there are tongues, they will be stilled; where there is knowledge, it will pass away. For we know in part and we prophesy in part, but when completeness comes, what is in part disappears. When I was a child, I talked like a child, I thought like a child, I reasoned like a child. When I became a man, I put the ways of childhood behind me. For now we see only a reflection as in a mirror; then we shall see face to face. Now I know in part; then I shall know fully, even as I am fully known.

And now these three remain: faith, hope and love. But the greatest of these is love."

John 15:11-13 "I have told you this so that my joy may be in you and that your joy may be complete. My command is this: Love each other as I have loved you. Greater love has no one than this: to lay down one's life for one's friends."

2 Thessalonians 3:5 (NKJV) "Now may the Lord direct your hearts into the love of God and into the patience of Christ."

Living a Holy Life

Psalm 148:1-2 "Praise the Lord.
Praise the Lord from the heavens;
    praise him in the heights above.
Praise him, all his angels;
    praise him, all his heavenly hosts."

Psalm 148:13 "Let them praise the name of the Lord,
    for his name alone is exalted;
    his splendor is above the earth and the heavens."

Psalm 139:23-24 "Search me, God, and know my heart;
    test me and know my anxious thoughts.
See if there is any offensive way in me,
    and lead me in the way everlasting."

Psalm 51:10-15 "Create in me a pure heart, O God,
    and renew a steadfast spirit within me.
Do not cast me from your presence
    or take your Holy Spirit from me.
Restore to me the joy of your salvation
    and grant me a willing spirit, to sustain me.
Then I will teach transgressors your ways,
    so that sinners will turn back to you.

Heavenly Father

Deliver me from the guilt of bloodshed, O God,
    you who are God my Savior,
    and my tongue will sing of your righteousness.
Open my lips, Lord,
    and my mouth will declare your praise."

Daniel 1:8 "But Daniel resolved not to defile himself with the royal food and wine, and he asked the chief official for permission not to defile himself this way."

Psalm 19:14 "May these words of my mouth and this
    meditation of my heart
    be pleasing in your sight,
    Lord, my Rock and my Redeemer."

Psalm 141:1-4 "I call to you, Lord, come quickly to me;
    hear me when I call to you.
May my prayer be set before you like incense;
    may the lifting up of my hands be like the evening sacrifice.
Set a guard over my mouth, Lord;
    keep watch over the door of my lips.
Do not let my heart be drawn to what is evil
    so that I take part in wicked deeds
along with those who are evildoers;
    do not let me eat their delicacies."

Philippians 1:6 "being confident of this, that he who began a good work in you will carry it on to completion until the day of Christ Jesus."

Philippians 1:9-11 "And this is my prayer: that your love may abound more and more in knowledge and depth of insight, so that you may be able to discern what is best and may be pure and blameless for the day of Christ, filled with the fruit of righteousness that comes through Jesus Christ—to the glory and praise of God."

1 Thessalonians 5:16-22 "Rejoice always, pray continually, give thanks in all circumstances; for this is God's will for you in Christ Jesus. Do not quench the Spirit. Do not treat prophecies with contempt but test them all; hold on to what is good, reject every kind of evil."

1 Chronicles 4:10 "Jabez cried out to the God of Israel, "Oh, that you would bless me and enlarge my territory! Let your hand be with me, and keep me from harm so that I will be free from pain." And God granted his request."

Jeremiah 33:3 "Call to me and I will answer you and tell you great and unsearchable things you do not know."

1 Corinthians 10:3-6 "They all ate the same spiritual food and drank the same spiritual drink; for they drank from the spiritual rock that accompanied them, and that rock was Christ. Nevertheless, God was not pleased with most of them; their bodies were scattered in the wilderness.

Now these things occurred as examples to keep us from setting our hearts on evil things as they did."

Hebrews 10:23 "Let us hold unswervingly to the hope we profess, for he who promised is faithful."

Hebrews 11:6 "And without faith it is impossible to please God, because anyone who comes to him must believe that he exists and that he rewards those who earnestly seek him."

Troubles and Suffering

Habakkuk 1:2-4 (NKJV) "O Lord, how long shall I cry,
And You will not hear?
Even cry out to You, "Violence!"
And You will not save.
Why do You show me iniquity,
And cause *me* to see trouble?
For plundering and violence *are* before me;
There is strife, and contention arises.
Therefore the law is powerless,
And justice never goes forth.
For the wicked surround the righteous;
Therefore perverse judgment proceeds."

Psalm 10:1-5 "Why, Lord, do you stand far off?
  Why do you hide yourself in times of trouble?

  In his arrogance the wicked man hunts down the weak,
    who are caught in the schemes he devises.
  He boasts about the cravings of his heart;
    he blesses the greedy and reviles the Lord.

> In his pride the wicked man does not seek him;
> > in all his thoughts there is no room for God.
> His ways are always prosperous;
> > your laws are rejected by him;
> > he sneers at all his enemies."

1 Peter 4:12-16 "Dear friends, do not be surprised at the fiery ordeal that has come on you to test you, as though something strange were happening to you. But rejoice inasmuch as you participate in the sufferings of Christ, so that you may be overjoyed when his glory is revealed. If you are insulted because of the name of Christ, you are blessed, for the Spirit of glory and of God rests on you. If you suffer, it should not be as a murderer or thief or any other kind of criminal, or even as a meddler. However, if you suffer as a Christian, do not be ashamed, but praise God that you bear that name."

1 Peter 5:6-9 "Humble yourselves, therefore, under God's mighty hand, that he may lift you up in due time. Cast all your anxiety on him because he cares for you.

Be alert and of sober mind. Your enemy the devil prowls around like a roaring lion looking for someone to devour. Resist him, standing firm in the faith, because you know that the family of believers throughout the world is undergoing the same kind of sufferings."

2 Peter 1:3-4 "His divine power has given us everything we need for a godly life through our knowledge of him who called us by his own glory and goodness. Through these he has given us his very great and precious promises, so that through them you may participate in the divine nature, having escaped the corruption in the world caused by evil desires."

Standing on God's Word

Micah 6:8 "He has shown you, O mortal, what is good.
　And what does the Lord require of you?
To act justly and to love mercy
　and to walk humbly with your God."

Micah 7:7 "But as for me, I watch in hope for the Lord,
　I wait for God my Savior;
　my God will hear me."

Lamentations 3:24, 26 "I say to myself,
"The Lord is my portion;
　therefore I will wait for him."
it is good to wait quietly
　for the salvation of the Lord."

2 Timothy 3:12-17 "In fact, everyone who wants to live a godly life in Christ Jesus will be persecuted, while evildoers and impostors will go from bad to worse, deceiving and being deceived. But as for you, continue in what you have learned and have become convinced of, because you know those from whom you learned it, and how from infancy you have known the Holy Scriptures, which are able to make you wise for salvation through faith in Christ Jesus. All Scripture is God-breathed and is useful for teaching, rebuking, correcting and training in righteousness, so that the servant of God may be thoroughly equipped for every good work."

Numbers 6:24-26 "The Lord bless you
    and keep you;
the Lord make his face shine on you
    and be gracious to you;
the Lord turn his face toward you
    and give you peace."

The Body of Christ

Colossians 1:9-23 "For this reason, since the day we heard about you, we have not stopped praying for you. We continually ask God to fill you with the knowledge of his will through all the wisdom and understanding that the Spirit gives, so that you may live a life worthy of the Lord and please him in every way: bearing fruit in every good work, growing in the knowledge of God, being strengthened with all power according to his glorious might so that you may have great endurance and patience, and giving joyful thanks to the Father, who has qualified you to share in the inheritance of his holy people in the kingdom of light. For he has rescued us from the dominion of darkness and brought us into the kingdom of the Son he loves, in whom we have redemption, the forgiveness of sins.

The Son is the image of the invisible God, the firstborn over all creation. For in him all things were created: things in heaven and on earth, visible and invisible, whether thrones or powers or rulers or authorities; all things have been created through him and for him. He is before all things, and in him all things hold together. And he is the head of the body, the church; he is the beginning and the firstborn from among the dead, so that in everything he might have the supremacy. For God was pleased to have all his fullness dwell in him, and through him to reconcile to himself all things, whether things on earth or things in heaven, by making peace through his blood, shed on the cross.

Once you were alienated from God and were enemies in your minds because of your evil behavior. But now he has reconciled you by Christ's physical body through death to present you holy in his sight, without blemish and free from accusation—if you continue in your faith, established and firm, and do not move from the hope held out in the gospel. This is the gospel that you heard and that has been proclaimed to every creature under heaven, and of which I, Paul, have become a servant."

The Church

Matthew 16:18-19 (NKJV) "And I also say to you that you are Peter, and on this rock I will build My church, and the gates of Hades shall not prevail against it. And I will give you the keys of the kingdom of heaven, and whatever you bind on earth will be bound in heaven, and whatever you loose on earth will be loosed in heaven."

Matthew 18:20 (NKJV) "For where two or three are gathered together in My name, I am there in the midst of them."

Acts 20:28 "Keep watch over yourselves and all the flock of which the Holy Spirit has made you overseers. Be shepherds of the church of God, which he bought with his own blood."

1 Thessalonians 5:12-13, 15-23 "Now we ask you, brothers and sisters, to acknowledge those who work hard among you, who care for you in the Lord and who admonish you. Hold them in the highest regard in love because of their work. Live in peace with each other.

"Make sure that nobody pays back wrong for wrong, but always strive to do what is good for each other and for everyone else.

Rejoice always, pray continually, give thanks in all circumstances; for this is God's will for you in Christ Jesus.

Do not quench the Spirit. Do not treat prophecies with contempt but test them all; hold on to what is good, reject every kind of evil.

May God himself, the God of peace, sanctify you through and through. May your whole spirit, soul and body be kept blameless at the coming of our Lord Jesus Christ."

School Districts

Colossians 3:12-17 "Therefore, as God's chosen people, holy and dearly loved, clothe yourselves with compassion, kindness, humility, gentleness and patience. Bear with each other and forgive one another if any of you has a grievance against someone. Forgive as the Lord forgave you. And over all these virtues put on love, which binds them all together in perfect unity.

Let the peace of Christ rule in your hearts, since as members of one body you were called to peace. And be thankful. Let the message of Christ dwell among you richly as you teach and admonish one another with all wisdom through psalms, hymns, and songs from the Spirit, singing to God with gratitude in your hearts. And whatever you do, whether in word or deed, do it all in the name of the Lord Jesus, giving thanks to God the Father through him."

Pursuing Wisdom

James 1:5 (NKJV) "If any of you lacks wisdom, let him ask of God, who gives to all liberally and without reproach, and it will be given to him."

2 Timothy 3:16-17 (NKJV) "All Scripture *is* given by inspiration of God, and *is* profitable for doctrine, for reproof, for correction, for instruction in righteousness, that the man of God may be complete, thoroughly equipped for every good work."

Proverbs 3:5-6 "Trust in the Lord with all your heart
 and lean not on your own understanding;
in all your ways submit to him,
 and he will make your paths straight."

Romans 15:2-6 "Each of us should please our neighbors for their good, to build them up. For even Christ did not please himself but, as it is written: "The insults of those who insult you have fallen on me." For everything that was written in the past was written to teach us, so that through the endurance taught in the Scriptures and the encouragement they provide we might have hope.

May the God who gives endurance and encouragement give you the same attitude of mind toward each other that Christ Jesus had, so that with one mind and one voice you may glorify the God and Father of our Lord Jesus Christ."

Matthew 7:7 "Ask and it will be given to you; seek and you will find; knock and the door will be opened to you."

1 Corinthians 15:58, 16:13 "Therefore, my dear brothers and sisters, stand firm. Let nothing move you. Always give yourselves fully to the work of the Lord, because you know that your labor in the Lord is not in vain."

"Be on your guard; stand firm in the faith; be courageous; be strong."

Joy in the Face of Trials

Psalm 13 "How long, Lord? Will you forget me forever?
　How long will you hide your face from me?
How long must I wrestle with my thoughts
　and day after day have sorrow in my heart?
　How long will my enemy triumph over me?

Look on me and answer, Lord my God.
　Give light to my eyes, or I will sleep in death,
and my enemy will say, "I have overcome him,"
　and my foes will rejoice when I fall.

But I trust in your unfailing love;
　my heart rejoices in your salvation.
I will sing the Lord's praise,
　for he has been good to me."

Habakkuk 1:2-4 "How long, Lord, must I call for help,
 but you do not listen?
Or cry out to you, "Violence!"
 but you do not save?
Why do you make me look at injustice?
 Why do you tolerate wrongdoing?
Destruction and violence are before me;
 there is strife, and conflict abounds.
Therefore the law is paralyzed,
 and justice never prevails.
The wicked hem in the righteous,
 so that justice is perverted."

Matthew 11:28-29 "Come to me, all you who are weary and burdened, and I will give you rest. Take my yoke upon you and learn from me, for I am gentle and humble in heart, and you will find rest for your souls."

James 1:2-4 "Consider it pure joy, my brothers and sisters, whenever you face trials of many kinds, because you know that the testing of your faith produces perseverance. Let perseverance finish its work so that you may be mature and complete, not lacking anything."

Hebrews 12:28-29 (The Message) "Do you see what we've got? An unshakable kingdom! And do you see how thankful we must be? Not only thankful, but brimming with worship, deeply reverent before God. For God is not an indifferent bystander. He's actively cleaning house, torching all that needs to burn, and he won't quit until it's all cleansed. God himself is Fire!"

Hebrews 13:5 "Keep your lives free from the love of money and be content with what you have, because God has said,

> "Never will I leave you;
> never will I forsake you."

Psalm 19:14 "May these words of my mouth and this
> meditation of my heart
> be pleasing in your sight,
> Lord, my Rock and my Redeemer."

Obedience to God

Ephesians 3:14-21 "For this reason I kneel before the Father, from whom every family in heaven and on earth derives its name. I pray that out of his glorious riches he may strengthen you with power through his Spirit in your inner being, so that Christ may dwell in your hearts through faith. And I pray that you, being rooted and established in love, may have power, together with all the Lord's holy people, to grasp how wide and long and high and deep is the love of Christ, and to know this love that surpasses knowledge—that you may be filled to the measure of all the fullness of God.

Now to him who is able to do immeasurably more than all we ask or imagine, according to his power that is at work within us, to him be glory in the church and in Christ Jesus throughout all generations, for ever and ever! Amen."

Romans 12:1-2 "Therefore, I urge you, brothers and sisters, in view of God's mercy, to offer your bodies as a living sacrifice, holy and pleasing to God—this is your true and proper worship. Do not conform to the pattern of this world, but be transformed by the renewing of your mind. Then you will be able to test and approve what God's will is—his good, pleasing and perfect will."

John 14:12-14 "Very truly I tell you, whoever believes in me will do the works I have been doing, and they will do even greater things than these, because I am going to the Father. And I will do whatever you ask in my name, so that the Father may be glorified in the Son. You may ask me for anything in my name, and I will do it."

1 Corinthians 15:58 "Therefore, my dear brothers and sisters, stand firm. Let nothing move you. Always give yourselves fully to the work of the Lord, because you know that your labor in the Lord is not in vain."

1 Corinthians 16:13 "Be on your guard; stand firm in the faith; be courageous; be strong."

1 Peter 3:15-16 "But in your hearts revere Christ as Lord. Always be prepared to give an answer to everyone who asks you to give the reason for the hope that you have. But do this with gentleness and respect, keeping a clear conscience, so that those who speak maliciously against your good behavior in Christ may be ashamed of their slander."

Philippians 1:9-11 "And this is my prayer: that your love may abound more and more in knowledge and depth of insight, so that you may be able to discern what is best and may be pure and blameless for the day of Christ, filled with the fruit of righteousness that comes through Jesus Christ—to the glory and praise of God."

Producing Good Fruit

Psalm 148:1-6 "Praise the Lord.

> Praise the Lord from the heavens;
> > praise him in the heights above.
> Praise him, all his angels;
> > praise him, all his heavenly hosts.
> Praise him, sun and moon;
> > praise him, all you shining stars.
> Praise him, you highest heavens
> > and you waters above the skies.

> Let them praise the name of the Lord,
> for at his command they were created,
> and he established them for ever and ever—
> he issued a decree that will never pass away."

1 Corinthians 13:4-7 "Love is patient, love is kind. It does not envy, it does not boast, it is not proud. It does not dishonor others, it is not self-seeking, it is not easily angered, it keeps no record of wrongs. Love does not delight in evil but rejoices with the truth. It always protects, always trusts, always hopes, always perseveres."

Matthew 5:44 "But I tell you, love your enemies and pray for those who persecute you"

Romans 8:37-39 "No, in all these things we are more than conquerors through him who loved us. For I am convinced that neither death nor life, neither angels nor demons, neither the present nor the future, nor any powers, neither height nor depth, nor anything else in all creation, will be able to separate us from the love of God that is in Christ Jesus our Lord."

Nehemiah 8:10 "Nehemiah said, "Go and enjoy choice food and sweet drinks, and send some to those who have nothing prepared. This day is holy to our Lord. Do not grieve, for the joy of the Lord is your strength."

Proverbs 10:1 "The proverbs of Solomon:

A wise son brings joy to his father,
   but a foolish son brings grief to his mother."

Proverbs 12:20 "Deceit is in the hearts of those who plot evil, but those who promote peace have joy."

John 16:24 "Until now you have not asked for anything in my name. Ask and you will receive, and your joy will be complete."

Romans 14:17-18 "For the kingdom of God is not a matter of eating and drinking, but of righteousness, peace and joy in the Holy Spirit, because anyone who serves Christ in this way is pleasing to God and receives human approval."

Philippians 1:4 "In all my prayers for all of you, I always pray with joy"

1 Thessalonians 5:16 "Rejoice always"

2 Thessalonians 3:16 "Now may the Lord of peace himself give you peace at all times and in every way. The Lord be with all of you."

1 Peter 3:8-12 "Finally, all of you, be like-minded, be sympathetic, love one another, be compassionate and humble. Do not repay evil with evil or insult with insult. On the contrary, repay evil with blessing, because to this you were called so that you may inherit a blessing. For,

> "Whoever would love life
>   and see good days
> must keep their tongue from evil
>   and their lips from deceitful speech.
> They must turn from evil and do good;
>   they must seek peace and pursue it.
> For the eyes of the Lord are on the righteous
>   and his ears are attentive to their prayer,
> but the face of the Lord is against those who do evil."

Philippians 4:7 "And the peace of God, which transcends all understanding, will guard your hearts and your minds in Christ Jesus."

Psalm 147:14 "He grants peace to your borders
   and satisfies you with the finest of wheat."

Proverbs 12:20 "Deceit is in the hearts of those who plot evil,
   but those who promote peace have joy."

Luke 1:79 "to shine on those living in darkness
   and in the shadow of death,
to guide our feet into the path of peace."

Matthew 5:9 "Blessed are the peacemakers,
   for they will be called children of God."

Proverbs 14:29 "Whoever is patient has great understanding, but one who is quick-tempered displays folly."

1 Thessalonians 5:14 "And we urge you, brothers and sisters, warn those who are idle and disruptive, encourage the disheartened, help the weak, be patient with everyone."

James 5:8-9 "You too, be patient and stand firm, because the Lord's coming is near. Don't grumble against one another, brothers and sisters, or you will be judged. The Judge is standing at the door!"

Romans 11:22 "Consider therefore the kindness and sternness of God: sternness to those who fell, but kindness to you, provided that you continue in his kindness. Otherwise, you also will be cut off."

Colossians 3:12 "Therefore, as God's chosen people, holy and dearly loved, clothe yourselves with compassion, kindness, humility, gentleness and patience."

2 Peter 1:7 "and to godliness, mutual affection; and to mutual affection, love."

Psalm 34:14 "Turn from evil and do good;
 seek peace and pursue it."

Psalm 112:5 "Good will come to those who are generous
 and lend freely,
 who conduct their affairs with justice."

Proverbs 3:27 "Do not withhold good from those to whom it is due,
when it is in your power to act."

Proverbs 11:27 "Whoever seeks good finds favor,
but evil comes to one who searches for it."

Proverbs 14:22 "Do not those who plot evil go astray? But those who plan what is good find love and faithfulness."

Matthew 13:8 "Still other seed fell on good soil, where it produced a crop—a hundred, sixty or thirty times what was sown."

Psalm 61:7 "May he be enthroned in God's presence forever;
appoint your love and faithfulness to protect him."

Psalm 86:15 "But you, Lord, are a compassionate and gracious God,
slow to anger, abounding in love and faithfulness."

Psalm 89:1 "I will sing of the Lord's great love forever;
with my mouth I will make your faithfulness known through all generations."

Philippians 4:5 "Let your gentleness be evident to all. The Lord is near."

Colossians 3:12 "Therefore, as God's chosen people, holy and dearly loved, clothe yourselves with compassion, kindness, humility, gentleness and patience."

1 Peter 3:15-16 "But in your hearts revere Christ as Lord. Always be prepared to give an answer to everyone who asks you to give the reason for the hope that you have. But do this with gentleness and respect, keeping a clear conscience, so that those who speak maliciously against your good behavior in Christ may be ashamed of their slander."

An Athlete's Prayer

Matthew 19:26 "Jesus looked at them and said, "With man this is impossible, but with God all things are possible."

Exercising your Body

Psalm 139:1 "You have searched me, Lord,
 and you know me."

Psalm 139:14 "I praise you because I am fearfully and
 wonderfully made;
 your works are wonderful,
 I know that full well."

Psalm 19:14 "May these words of my mouth and this
 meditation of my heart

be pleasing in your sight,
Lord, my Rock and my Redeemer."

Romans 12:1-2 "Therefore, I urge you, brothers and sisters, in view of God's mercy, to offer your bodies as a living sacrifice, holy and pleasing to God—this is your true and proper worship. Do not conform to the pattern of this world, but be transformed by the renewing of your mind. Then you will be able to test and approve what God's will is—his good, pleasing and perfect will."

1 John 4:4 "You, dear children, are from God and have overcome them, because the one who is in you is greater than the one who is in the world."

Isaiah 40:29 "He gives strength to the weary
and increases the power of the weak."

Philippians 4:13 "I can do all this through him who gives me strength."

Romans 8:37 "No, in all these things we are more than conquerors through him who loved us."

Psalm 59:16-17 "But I will sing of your strength,
in the morning I will sing of your love;
for you are my fortress,
my refuge in times of trouble.

> You are my strength, I sing praise to you;
> you, God, are my fortress,
> my God on whom I can rely."

Handling Money

Malachi 3:10 MEV "Bring all the tithes into the storehouse, that there may be food in My house, and test Me now in this, says the Lord of Hosts, if I will not open for you the windows of heaven and pour out for you a blessing, that *there will* not *be room* enough *to receive it.*"

Acts 20:35 "In everything I did, I showed you that by this kind of hard work we must help the weak, remembering the words the Lord Jesus himself said: 'It is more blessed to give than to receive.'"

2 Corinthians 9:7 "Each of you should give what you have decided in your heart to give, not reluctantly or under compulsion, for God loves a cheerful giver."

Matthew 6:19-21 "Do not store up for yourselves treasures on earth, where moths and vermin destroy, and where thieves break in and steal. But store up for yourselves treasures in heaven, where moths and vermin do not destroy, and where thieves do not break in and steal. For where your treasure is, there your heart will be also."

Physical and Mental Health

Psalm 139:13-16 "For you created my inmost being;
  you knit me together in my mother's womb.
I praise you because I am fearfully and wonderfully made;
  your works are wonderful,
  I know that full well.
My frame was not hidden from you
  when I was made in the secret place,
  when I was woven together in the depths of the earth.
Your eyes saw my unformed body;
  all the days ordained for me were written in your book
  before one of them came to be."

James 5:13-15 (NKJV) "Is anyone among you suffering? Let him pray. Is anyone cheerful? Let him sing psalms. Is anyone among you sick? Let him call for the elders of the church, and let them pray over him, anointing him with oil in the name of the Lord. And the prayer of faith will save the sick, and the Lord will raise him up. And if he has committed sins, he will be forgiven."

James 5:16 "Therefore confess your sins to each other and pray for each other so that you may be healed. The prayer of a righteous person is powerful and effective."

1 Peter 5:6-11 "Humble yourselves, therefore, under God's mighty hand, that he may lift you up in due time. Cast all your anxiety on him because he cares for you.

Be alert and of sober mind. Your enemy the devil prowls around like a roaring lion looking for someone to devour. Resist him, standing firm in the faith, because you know that the family of believers throughout the world is undergoing the same kind of sufferings.

And the God of all grace, who called you to his eternal glory in Christ, after you have suffered a little while, will himself restore you and make you strong, firm and steadfast. To him be the power for ever and ever. Amen."

Leading People

Romans 15:2-6 (NKJV) "Let each of us please *his* neighbor for *his* good, leading to edification. For even Christ did not please Himself; but as it is written, "The reproaches of those who reproached You fell on Me." For whatever things were written before were written for our learning, that we through the patience and comfort of the Scriptures might have hope. Now may the God of patience and comfort grant you to be like-minded toward one another, according to Christ Jesus, that you may with one mind *and* one mouth glorify the God and Father of our Lord Jesus Christ."